Bond

Non-verbal Reasoning
Assessment Papers

**9–10 years
Book 2**

Nic Morgan

Great Clarendon Street, Oxford, OX2 6DP, United Kingdom

Oxford University Press is a department of the University of Oxford. It furthers the University's objective of excellence in research, scholarship, and education by publishing worldwide. Oxford is a registered trade mark of Oxford University Press in the UK and in certain other countries

© Nic Morgan 2007, 2013
Illustrations © Oxford University Press

The moral rights of the author have been asserted

First published in 2007 by Nelson Thornes Ltd
This edition published in 2014

All rights reserved. No part of this publication may be reproduced, stored in a retrieval system, or transmitted, in any form or by any means, without the prior permission in writing of Oxford University Press, or as expressly permitted by law, by licence or under terms agreed with the appropriate reprographics rights organization. Enquiries concerning reproduction outside the scope of the above should be sent to the Rights Department, Oxford University Press, at the address above.

You must not circulate this work in any other form and you must impose this same condition on any acquirer

British Library Cataloguing in Publication Data
Data available

978-1-4085-2524-1

10 9 8 7 6 5 4 3 2 1

Printed in China

Acknowledgements

Page make-up: OKS Prepress, India
Illustrations: Bede Illustration

Before you get started

What is Bond?

This book is part of the Bond Assessment Papers series for non-verbal reasoning, which provides a **thorough and progressive course in non-verbal reasoning** from ages six to twelve. It builds up non-verbal reasoning skills from book to book over the course of the series.

What does this book cover and how can it be used to prepare for exams?

Non-verbal reasoning questions can be grouped into four distinct groups: identifying shapes, missing shapes, rotating shapes, and coded shapes and logic. *Non-verbal Reasoning 9–10 Book 1* and *Book 2* practise a wide range of questions appropriate to the age group drawn from all these categories. The papers can be used both for general practice and as part of the run-up to 11+ and other selective exams. One of the key features of Bond Assessment Papers is that each one practises **a very wide variety of skills and question types** so that children are always challenged to think – and don't get bored repeating the same question type again and again. We believe that variety is the key to effective learning. It helps children 'think on their feet' and cope with the unexpected: it is surprising how often children come out of non-verbal reasoning exams having met question types they have not seen before.

What does the book contain?

- **6 papers** – each one contains 54 questions.
- **Tutorial links throughout** – 📖 – this icon appears next to the questions. It indicates links to the relevant section in *How to do . . . 11+ Non-verbal Reasoning*, our invaluable subject guide that offers explanations and practice for all core question types.
- **Scoring devices** – there are score boxes at the end of each paper and a Progress Chart on page 56. The chart is a visual and motivating way for children to see how they are doing. It also turns the score into a percentage that can help decide what to do next.
- **Next Steps Planner** – advice on what to do after finishing the papers can be found on the inside back cover.
- **Answers** – located in an easily-removed central pull-out section.

How can you use this book?

One of the great strengths of Bond Assessment Papers is their flexibility. They can be used at home, in school and by tutors to:

- set **timed formal practice** tests – allow about 40 minutes per paper. Reduce the suggested time limit by five minutes to practise working at speed.

- provide **bite-sized chunks** for regular practice
- **highlight strengths and weaknesses** in the core skills
- identify **individual needs**
- set **homework**
- follow a **complete 11+ preparation strategy** alongside *The Parents' Guide to the 11+* (see below).

It is best to start at the beginning and work through the papers in order. If you are using the book as part of a careful run-in to the 11+, we suggest that you also have two other essential Bond resources close at hand:

How to do . . . 11+ Non-verbal Reasoning: the subject guide that explains all the question types practised in this book. Use the cross-reference icons to find the relevant sections.

The Parents' Guide to the 11+: the step-by-step guide to the whole 11+ experience. It clearly explains the 11+ process, provides guidance on how to assess children, helps you to set complete action plans for practice and explains how you can use *Non-verbal Reasoning 9–10 Book 1* and *Book 2* as part of a strategic run-in to the exam.

See the inside front cover for more details of these books.

What does a score mean and how can it be improved?

It is unfortunately impossible to predict how a child will perform when it comes to the 11+ (or similar) exam if they achieve a certain score on any practice book or paper. Success on the day depends on a host of factors, including the scores of the other children sitting the test. However, we can give some guidance on what a score indicates and how to improve it.

If children colour in the Progress Chart on page 56, this will give an idea of present performance in percentage terms. The Next Steps Planner inside the back cover will help you to decide what to do next to help a child progress. It is always valuable to go over wrong answers with children. If they are having trouble with any particular question type, follow the tutorial links to *How to do . . . 11+ Non-verbal Reasoning* for step-by-step explanations and further practice.

Don't forget the website . . . !

Visit www.bond11plus.co.uk for lots of advice, information and suggestions on everything to do with Bond, the 11+ and helping children to do their best.

Paper 1

B1 Which is the odd one out? Circle the letter.

Example

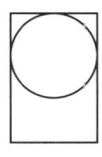  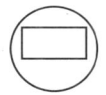 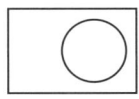 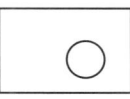

a   b   (c)   d   e

1.   

a   b   (c)   d   e

2. 

a   (b)   c   d   e

3. 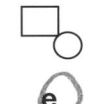

a   b   c   d   (e)

4. 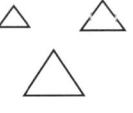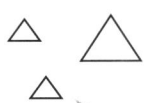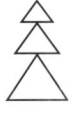

a   (b)   c   d   e

5. 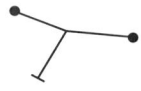

(a)   b   c   d   e

6. 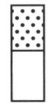

a   b   c   d   (e)

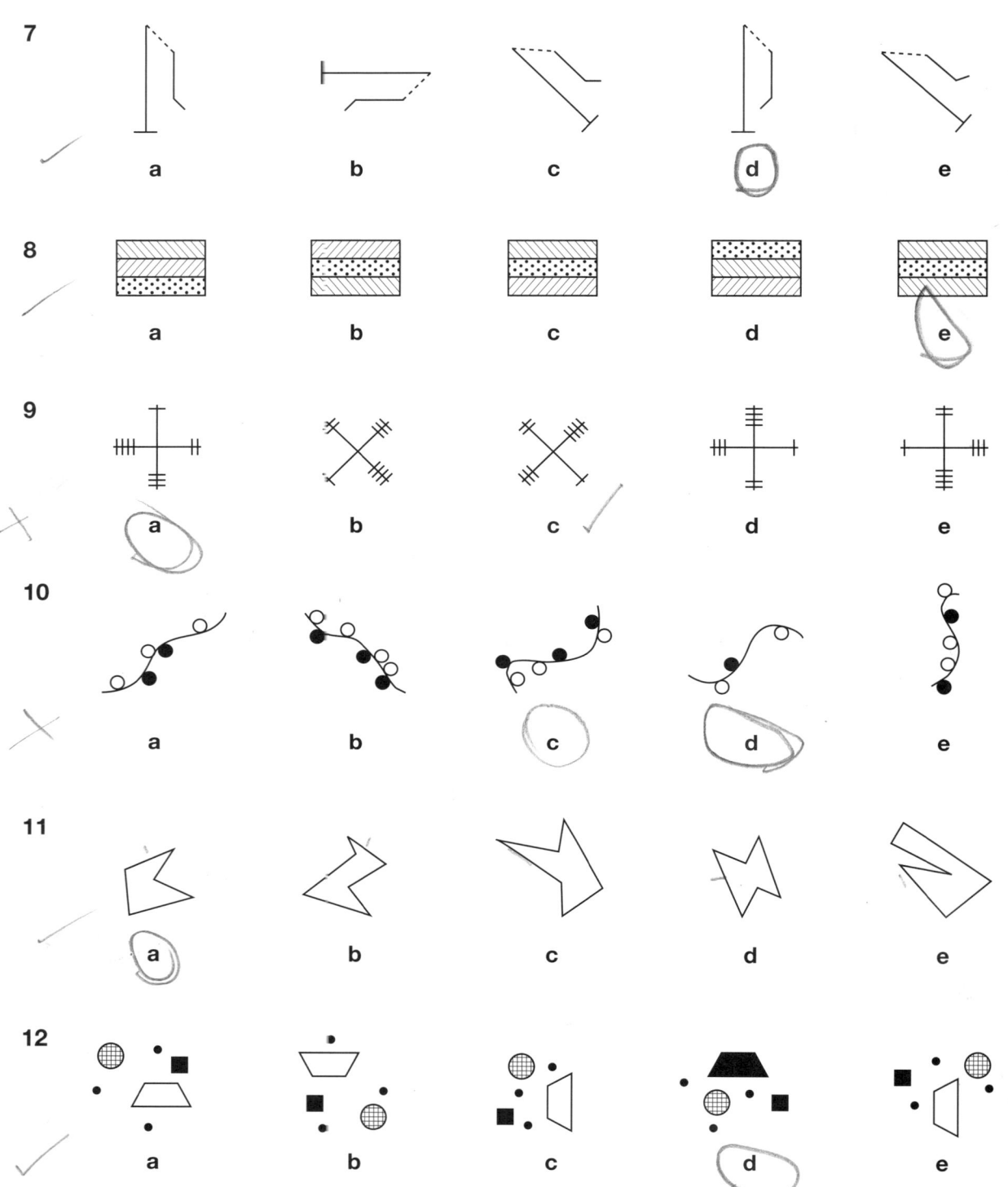

Which one comes next? Circle the letter.

Example

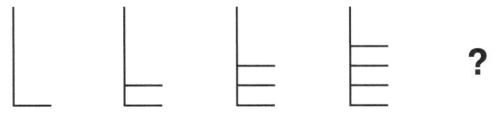 ?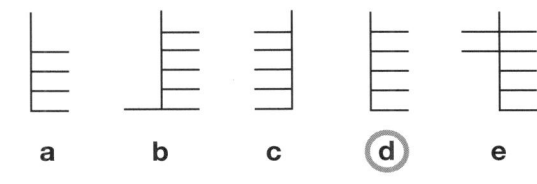

a b c (d) e

13 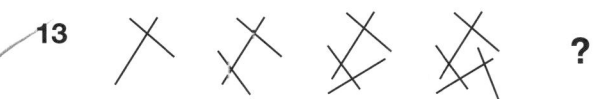 ?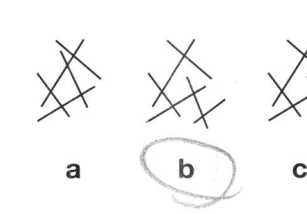

a b c d e

14 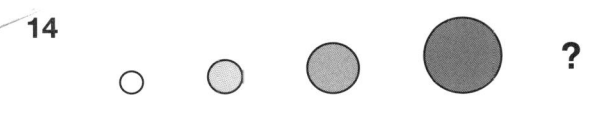 ?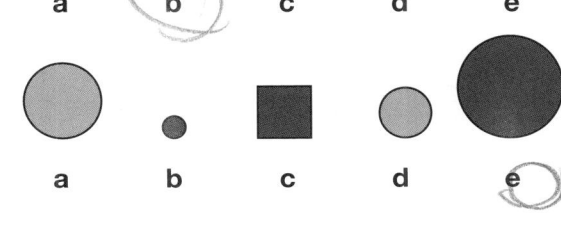

a b c d e

15  ?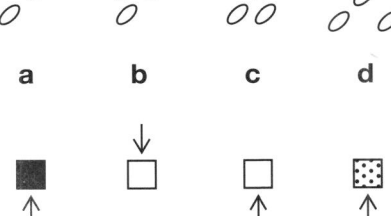

a b c d e

16 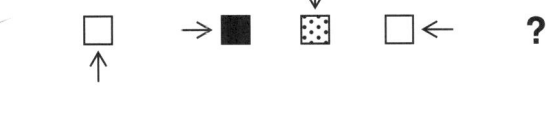 ?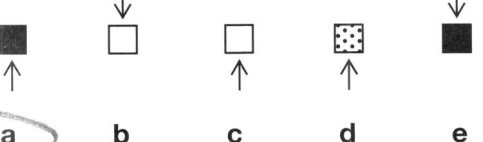

a b c d e

17 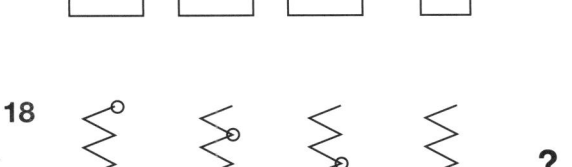 ?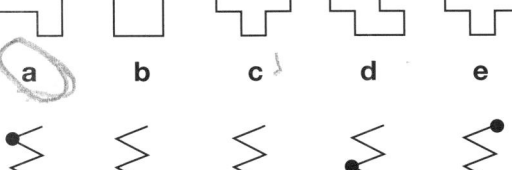

a b c d e

18  ?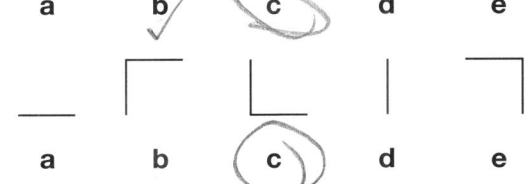

a b c d e

19

a b c d e

3

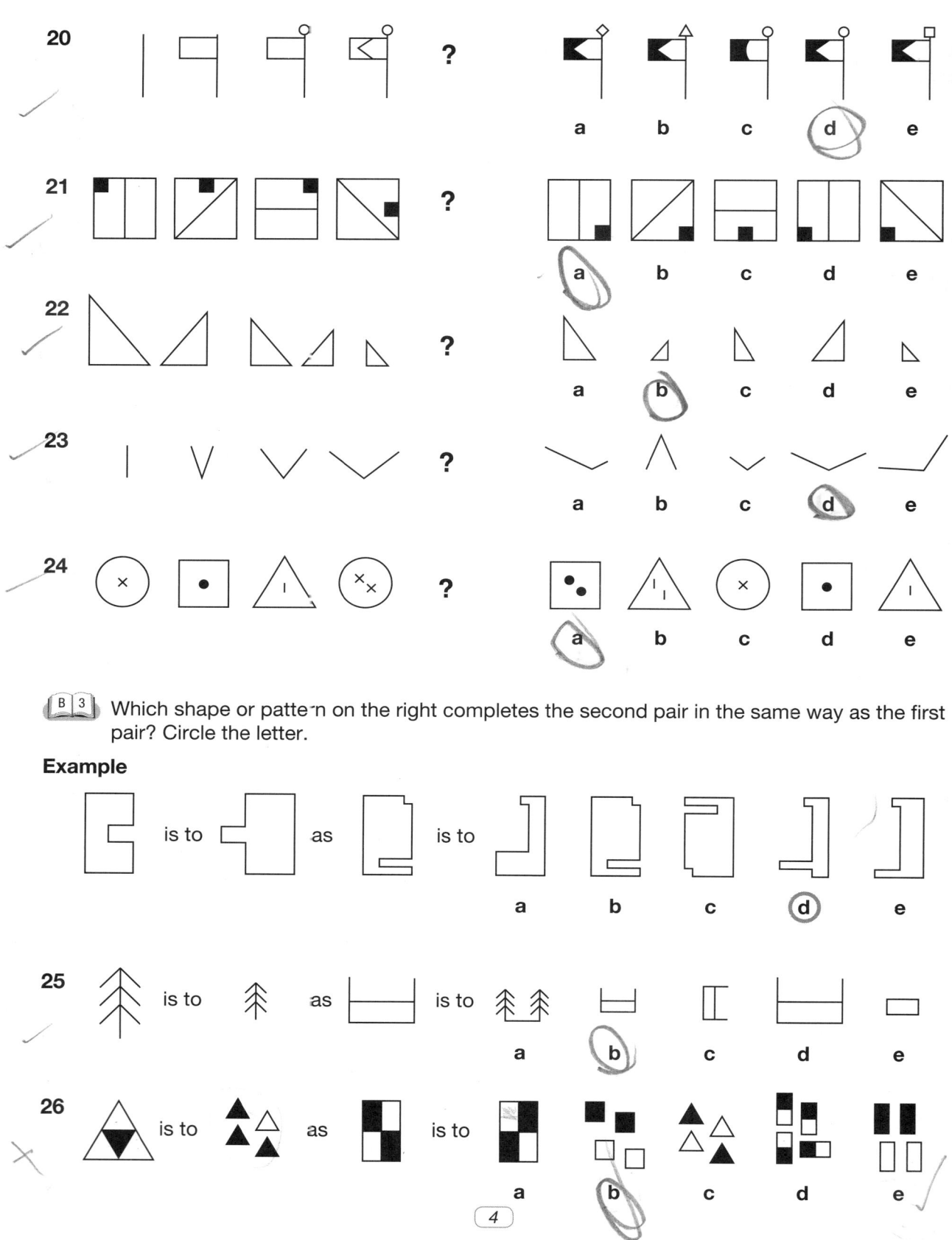

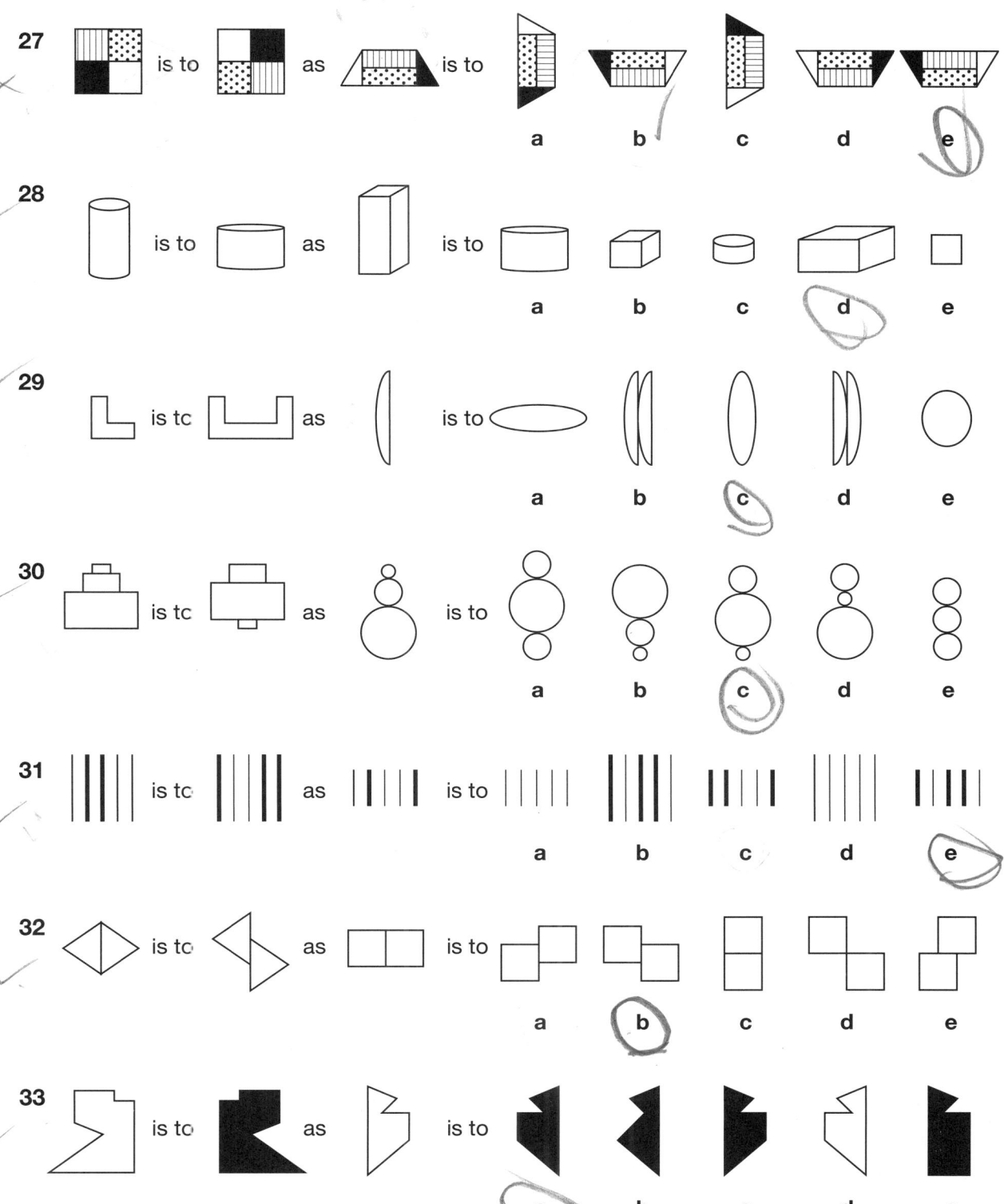

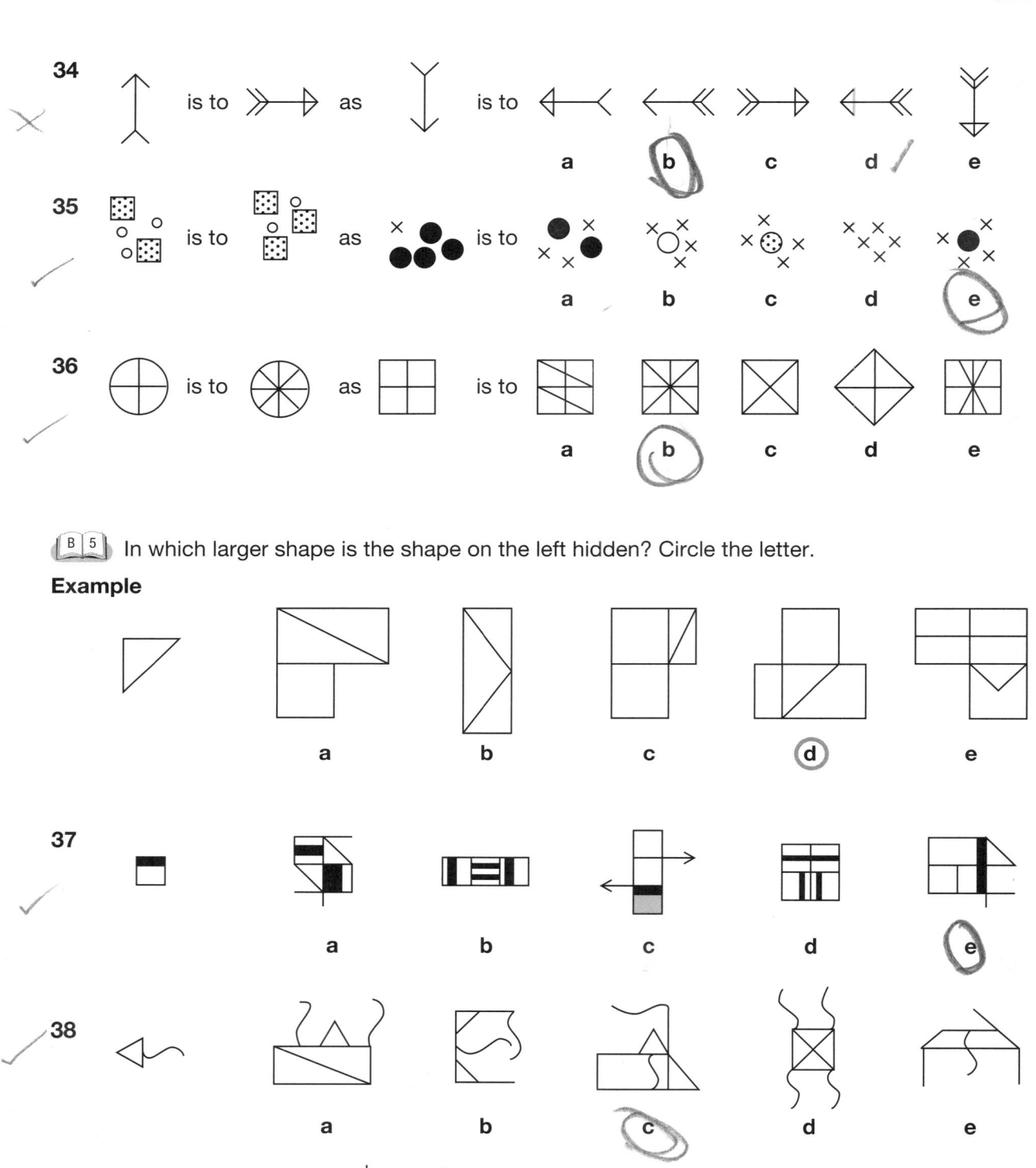

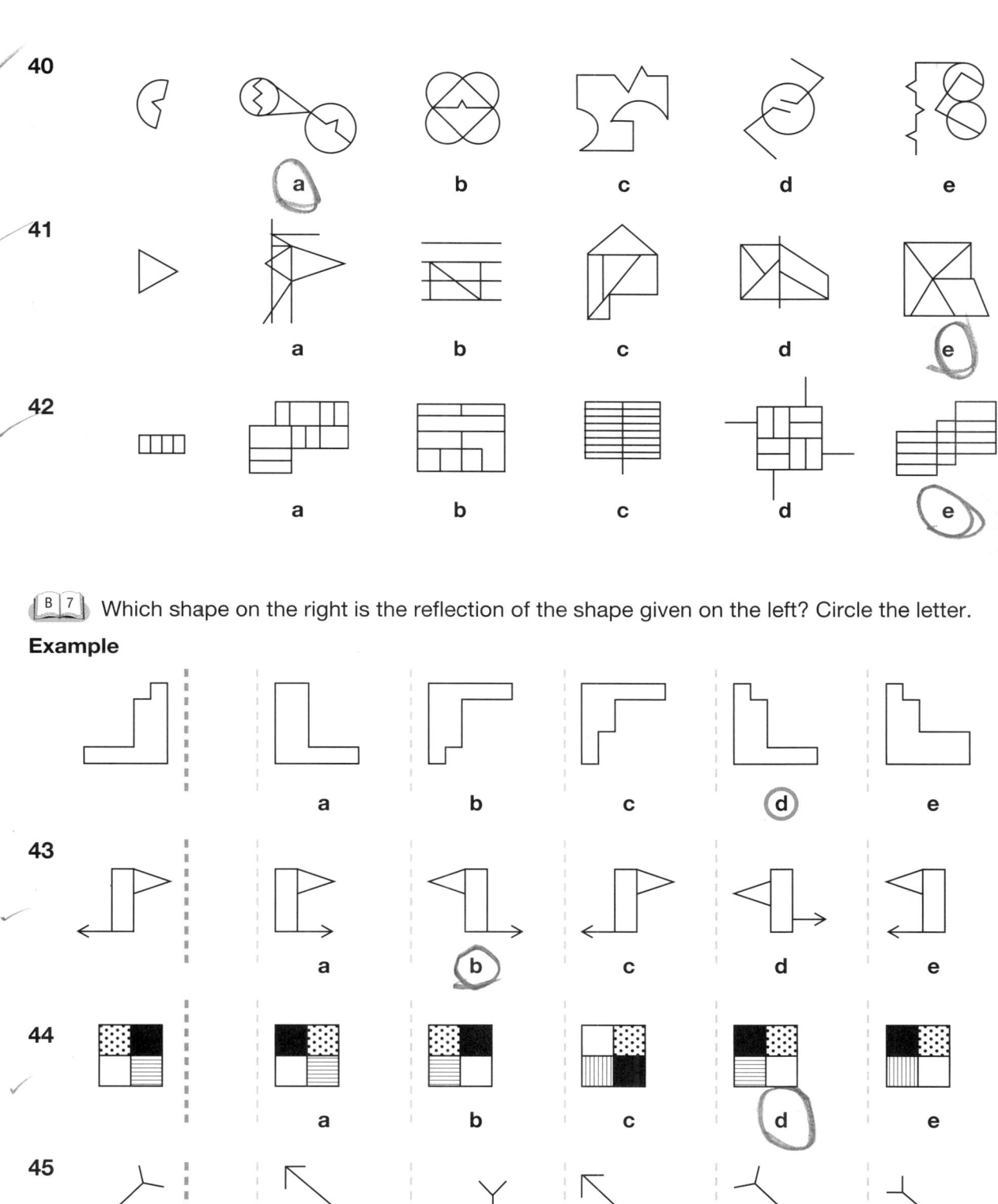

46

a b c d e

47

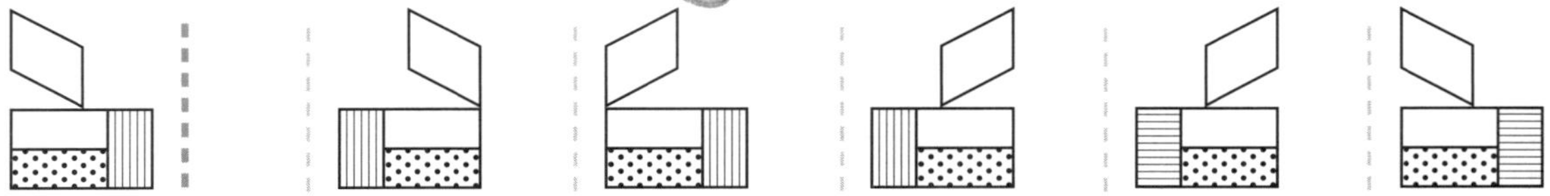

a b c d e

48

a b c d e

Which code matches the shape or pattern given at the end of each line? Circle the letter.

Example

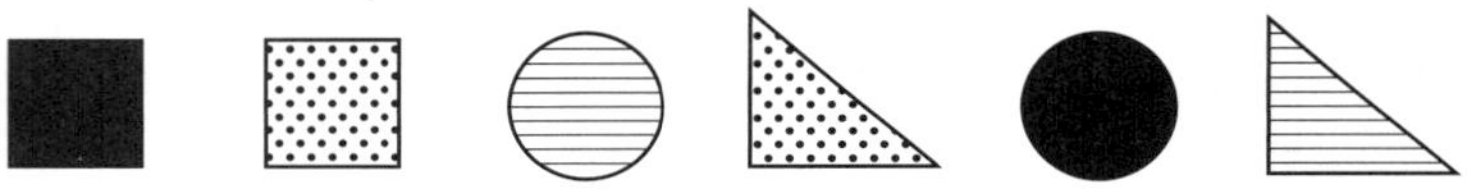

AX AY BZ CY BX ?   BZ AZ CX BY CZ
                          a   b   c   d   e

49

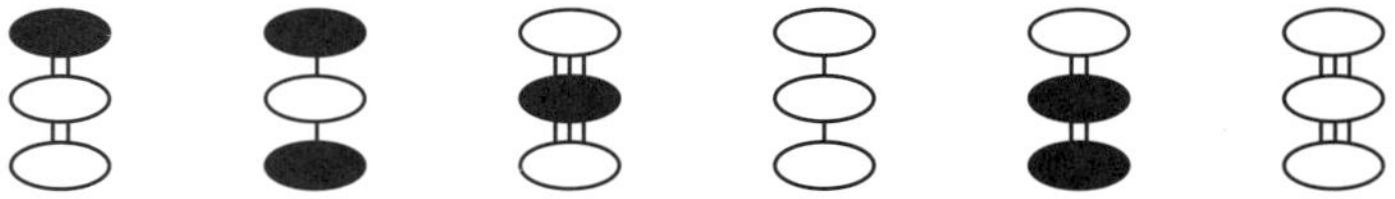

QE PF RE PD QF ?   RF QD PD PE RD
                          a   b   c   d   e

50

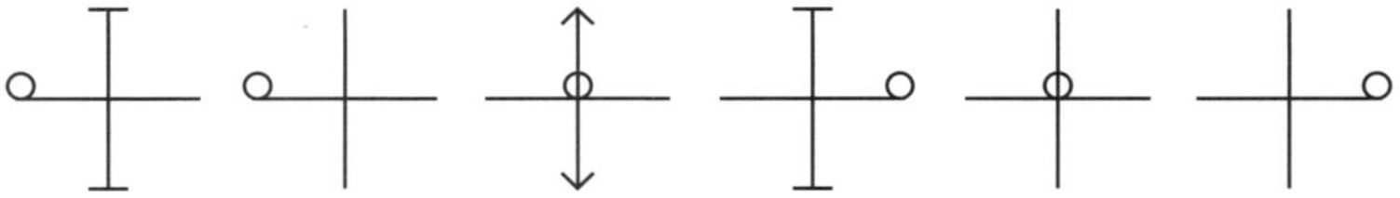

MU LU NV MW LV ?   MV NU LW LU NW
                          a   b   c   d   e

51

FA HC GB GC FB ?   HB HA FC GA HC
                          a   b   c   d   e

52 TJ SK TL UK SJ ?   UL SL UJ SJ TK
                              a   b   c   d   e

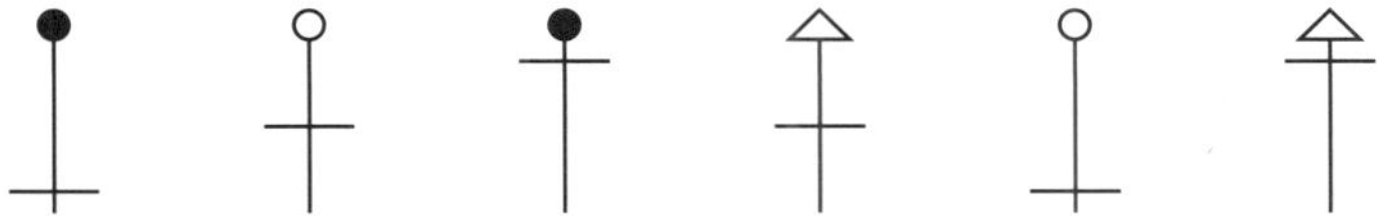

53 EX CZ DZ EY DX ?   DY EZ CX CZ CY
                              a   b   c   d   e

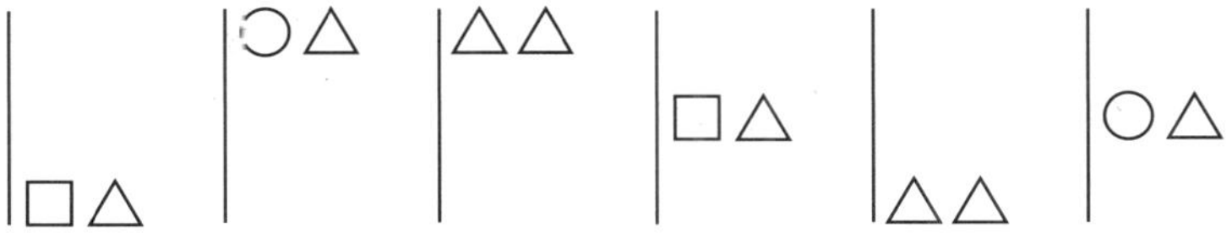

54 DR DU BS CR BT ?   CS BU DS CU DT
                              a   b   c   d   e

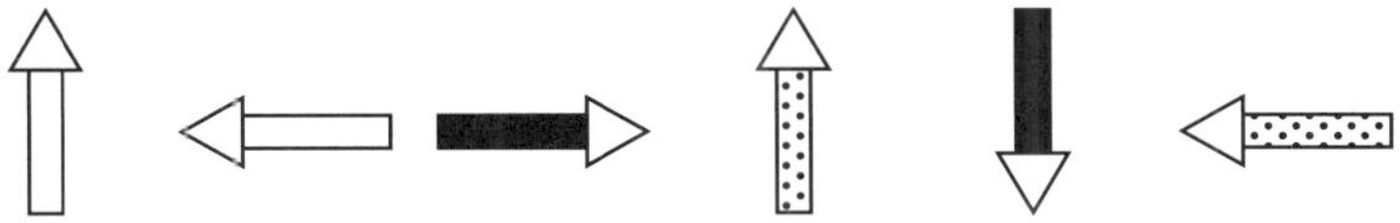

Now go to the Progress Chart to record your score! Total 45 / 54

82%

Paper 2

1 Which is the odd one out? Circle the letter.

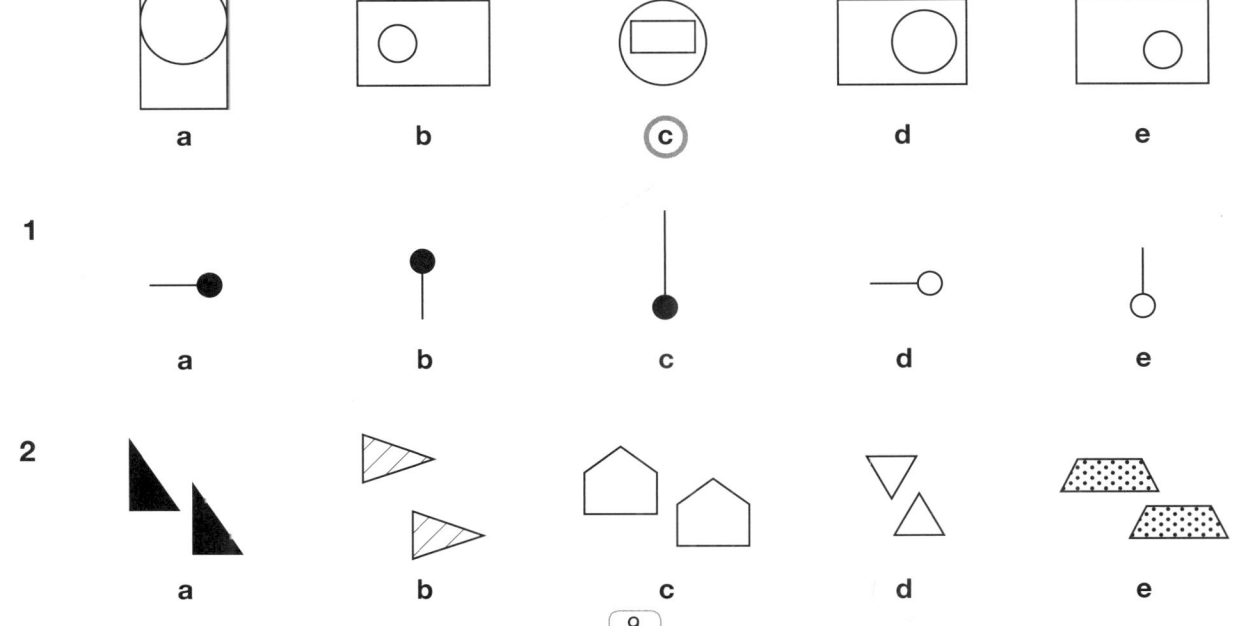

Example

a   b   c   d   e

1

a   b   c   d   e

2

a   b   c   d   e

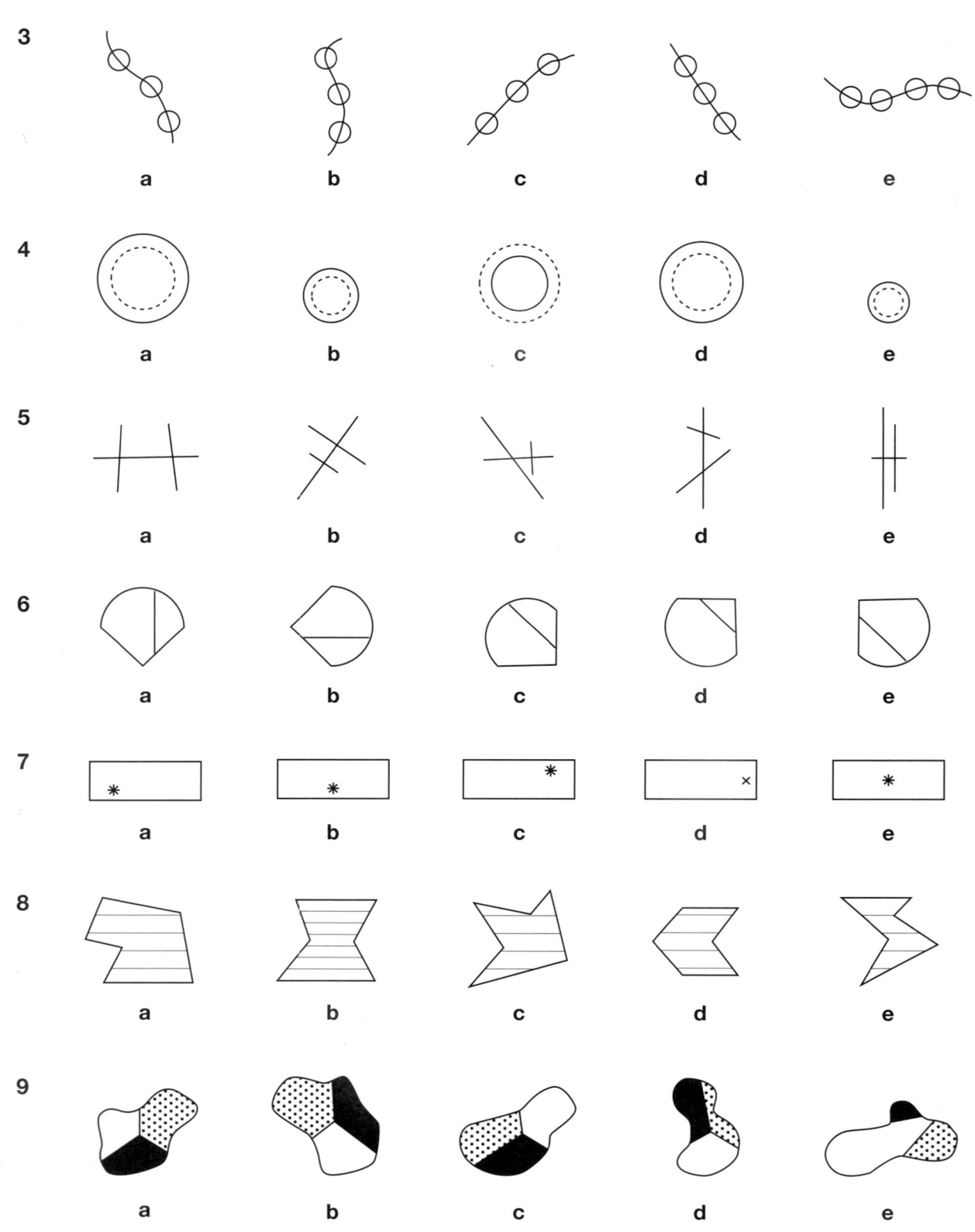

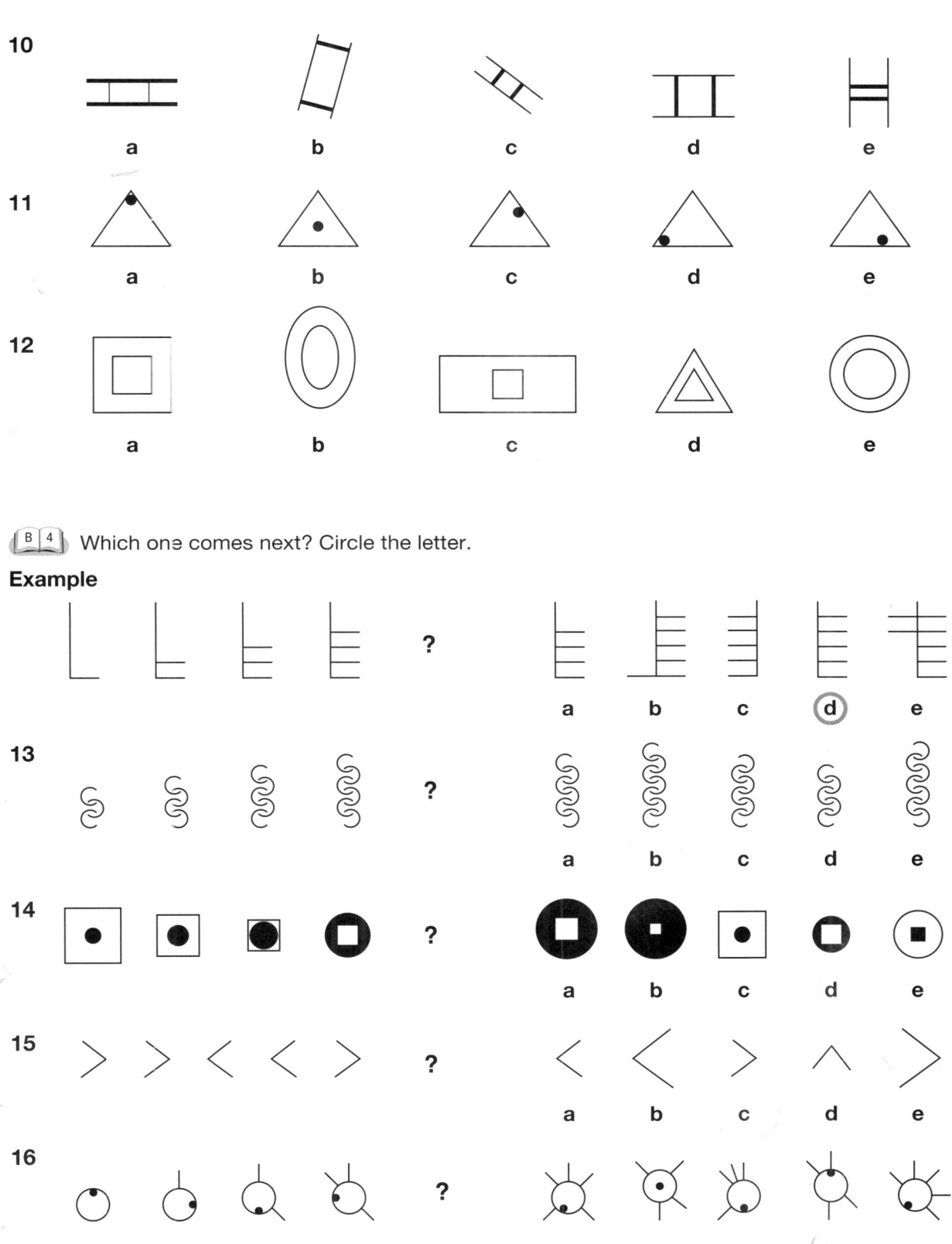

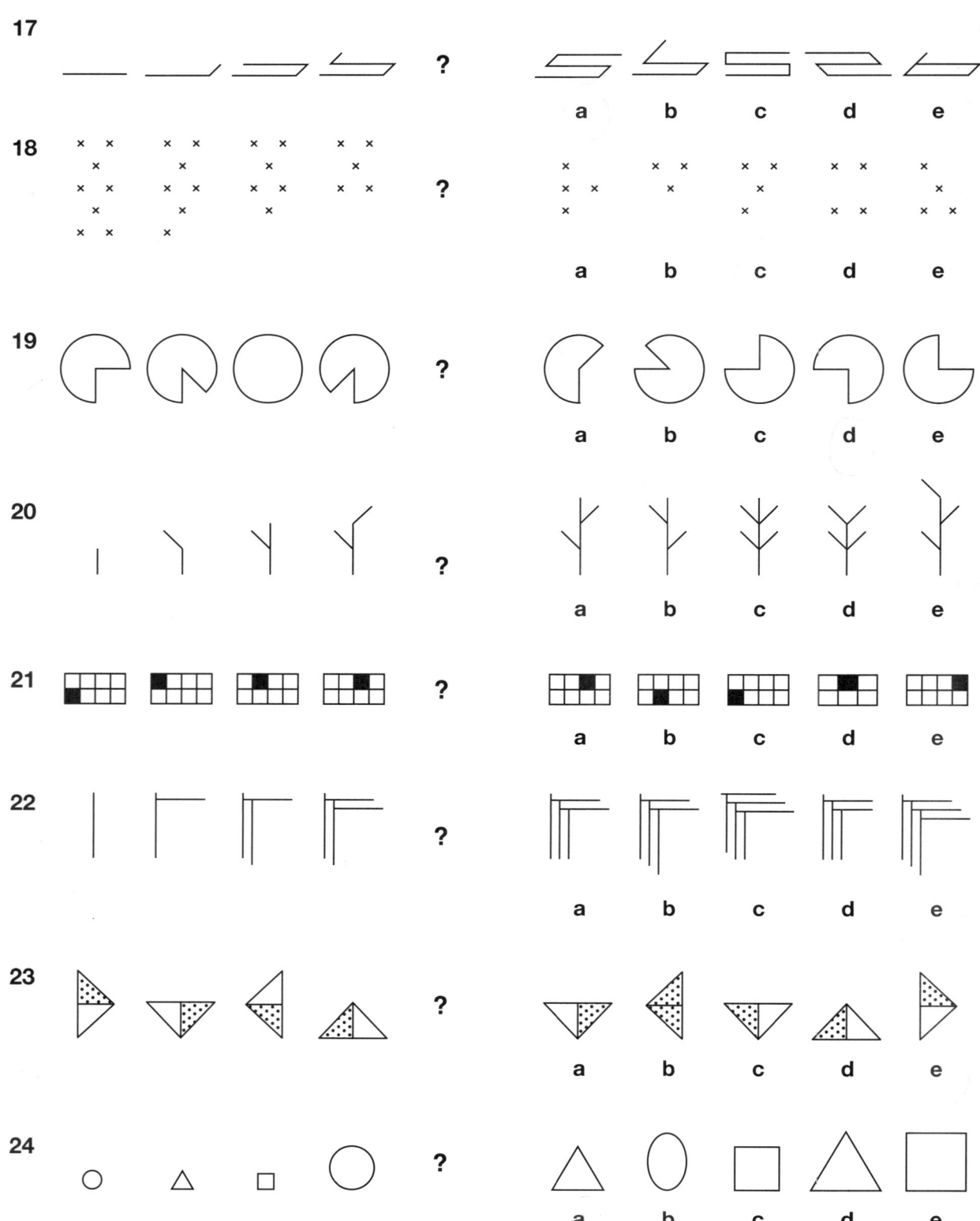

B3 Which shape or pattern on the right completes the second pair in the same way as the first pair? Circle the letter.

Example

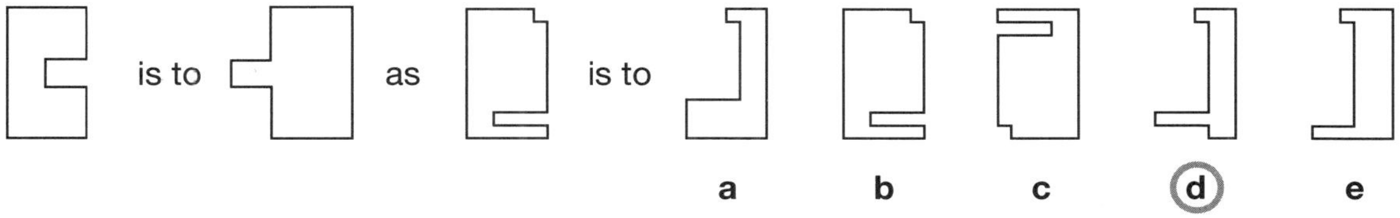

[Example showing shape is to shape as shape is to options a, b, c, d, e — with **d** circled]

25 [shape is to shape as shape is to options a–e]

26 [shape is to shape as shape is to options a–e]

27 [pattern is to pattern as pattern is to options a–e]

28 [square is to rectangle as triangle is to options a–e]

29 [arrow is to shape as arrow is to options a–e]

30 [line is to rectangle as shape is to options a–e]

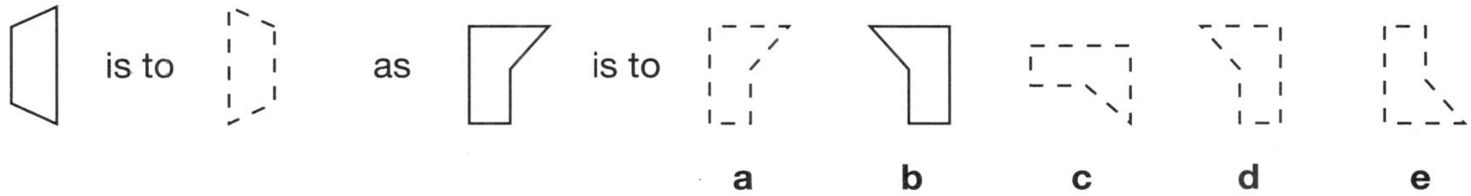

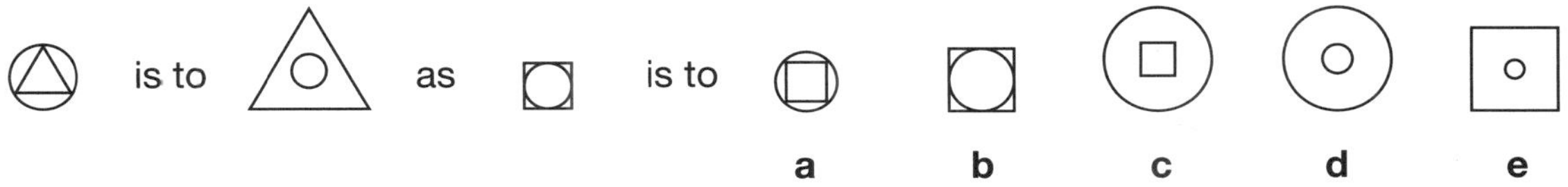

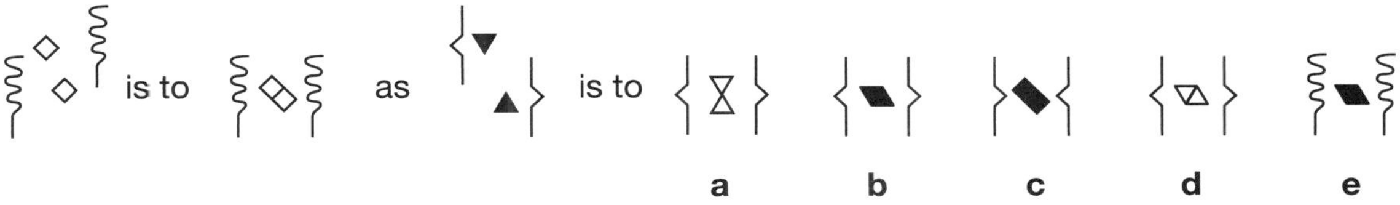

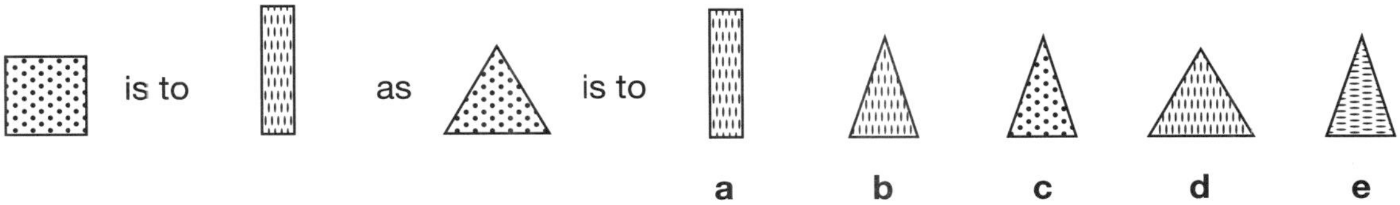

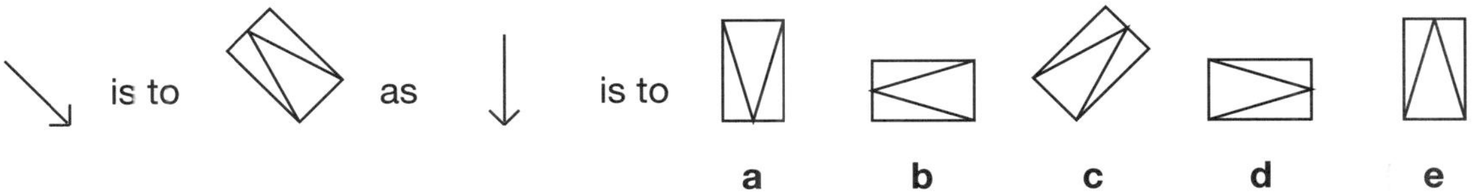

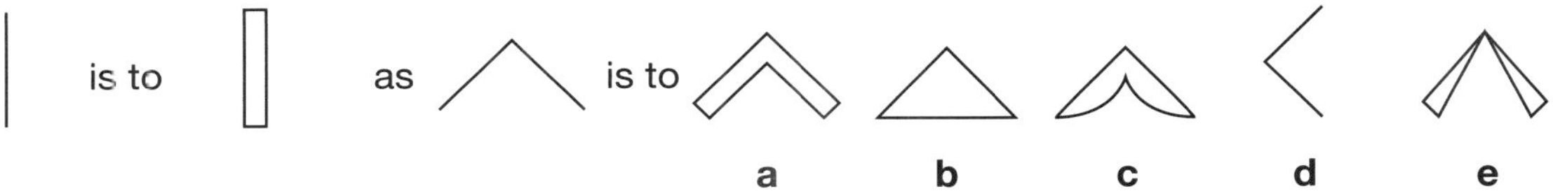

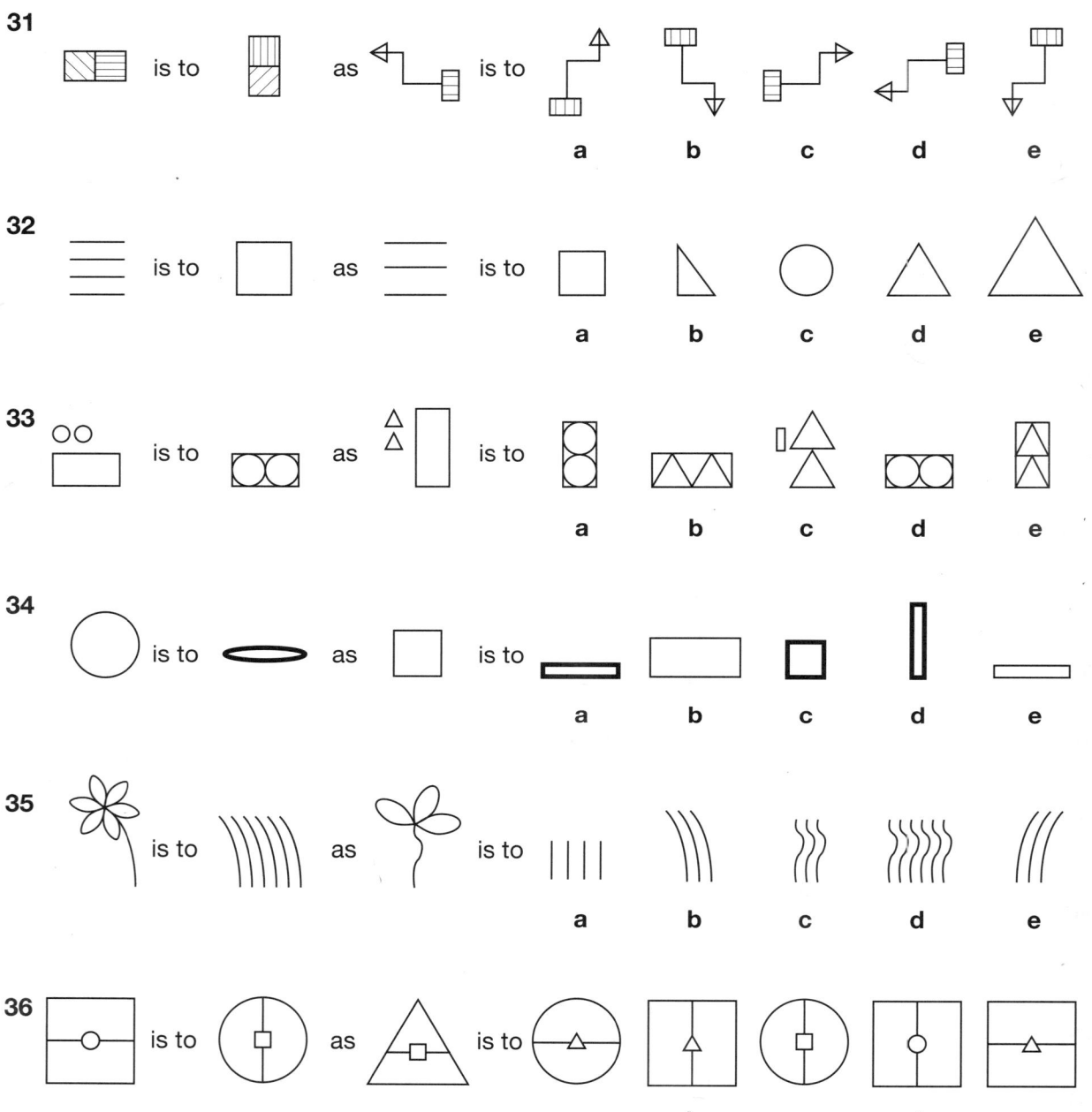

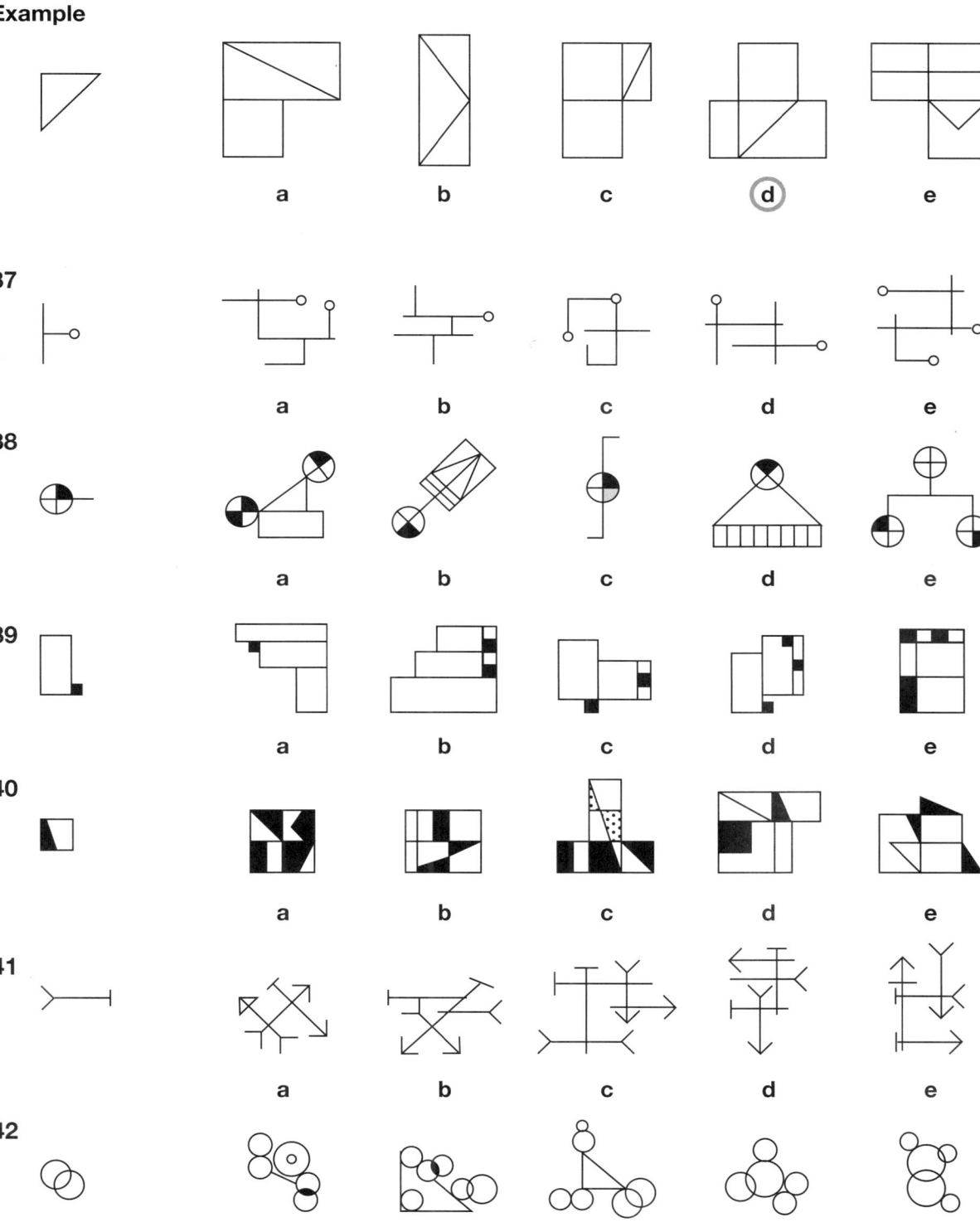

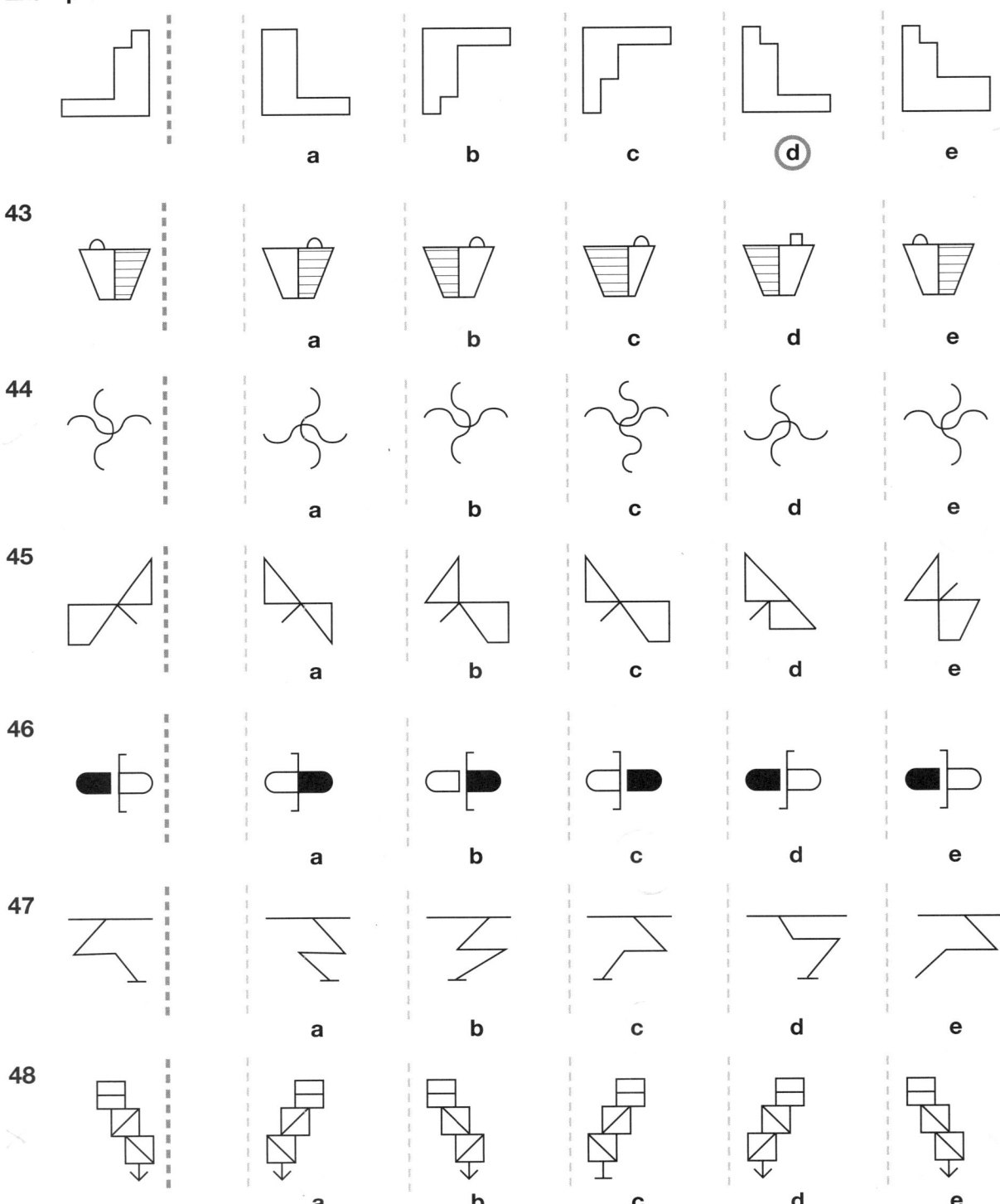

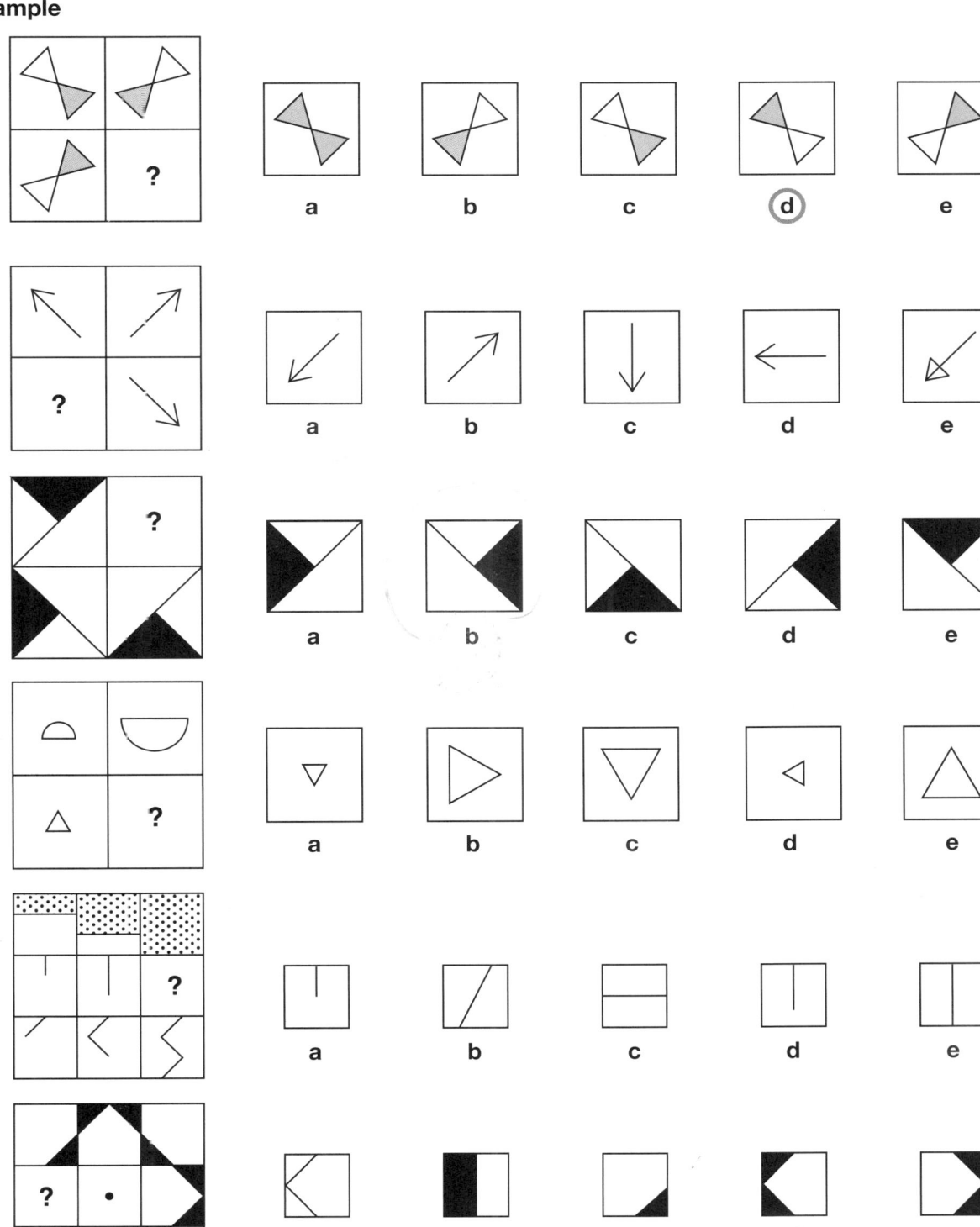

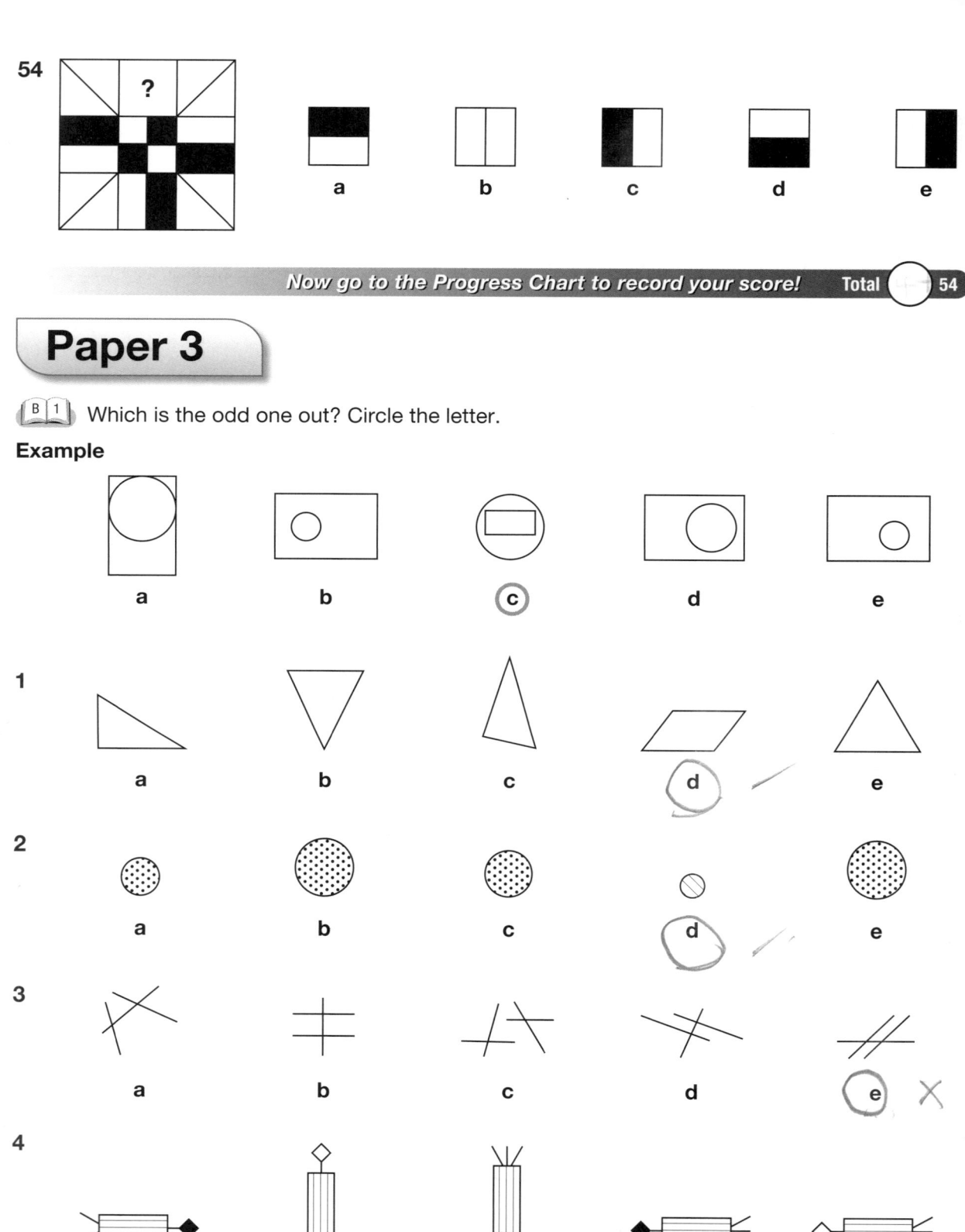

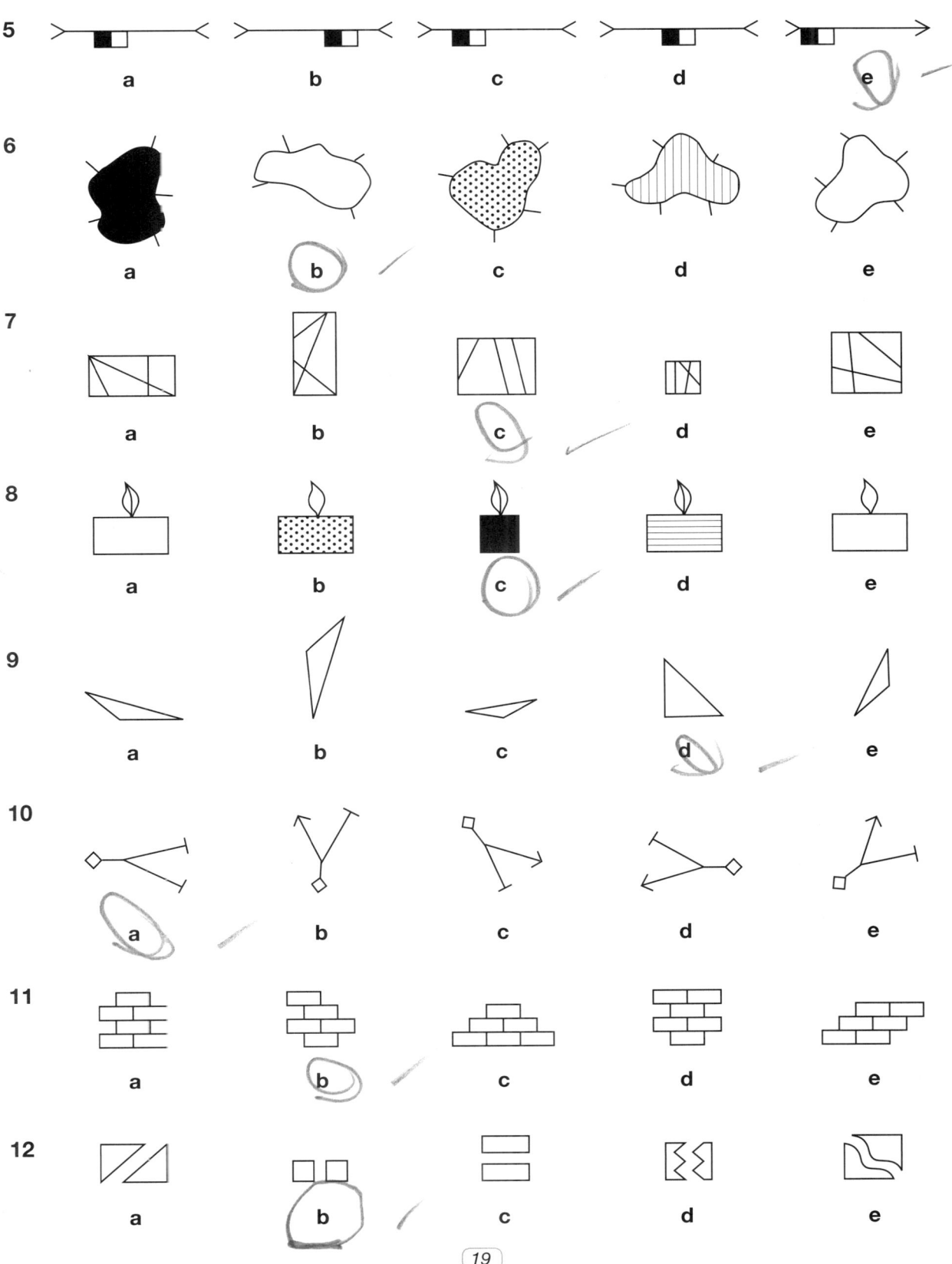

 Which one comes next? Circle the letter.

Example

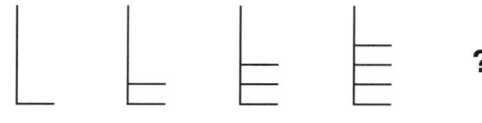 ?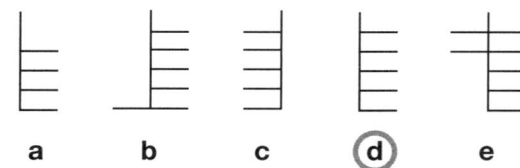
a b c (d) e

13  ?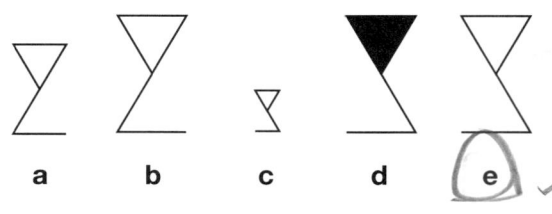
a b c d (e) ✓

14  ?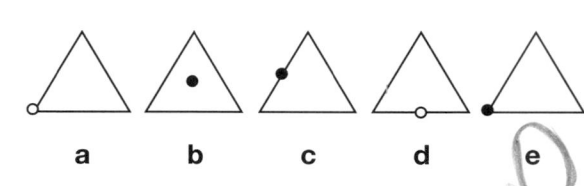
a b c d (e) ✓

15 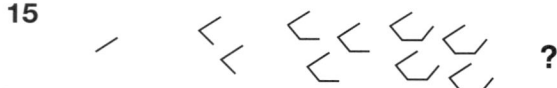 ?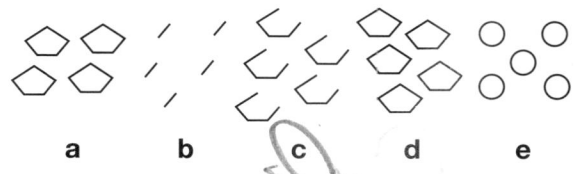
a b (c) d e ✗

16 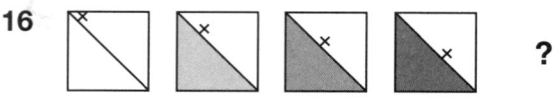 ?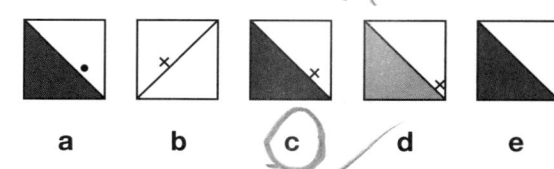
a b (c) ✓ d e

17 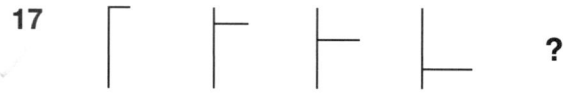 ?
a (b) ✓ c d e

18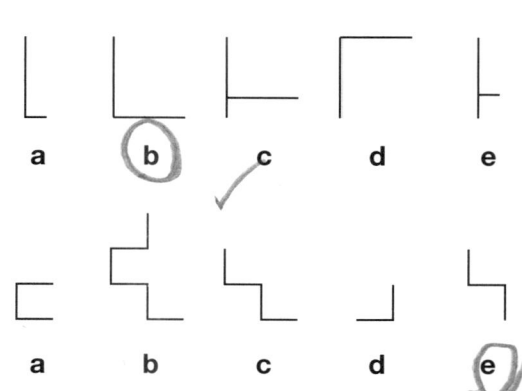
a b c d (e) ✗

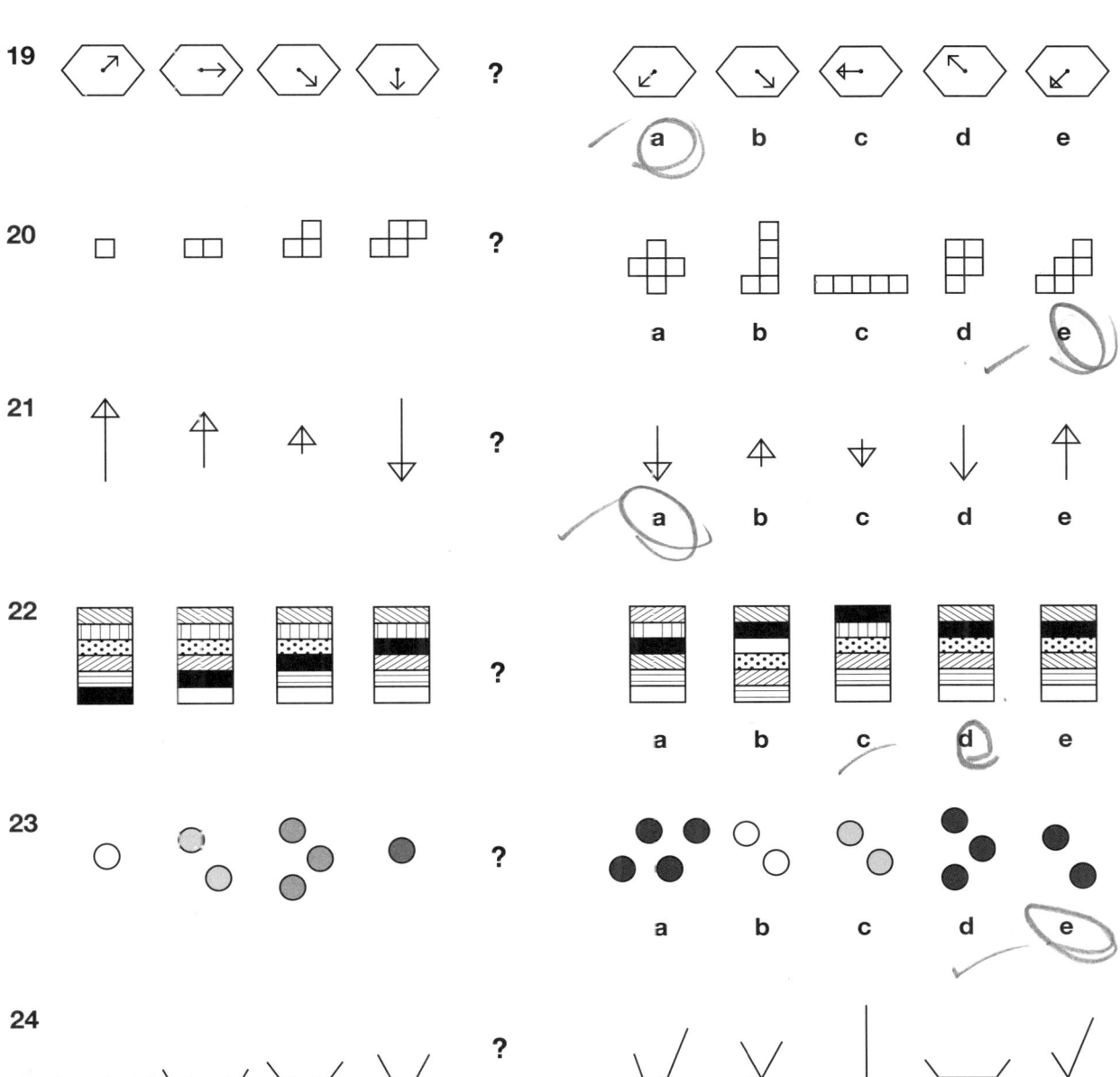

B3 Which shape or pattern on the right completes the second pair in the same way as the first pair? Circle the letter.

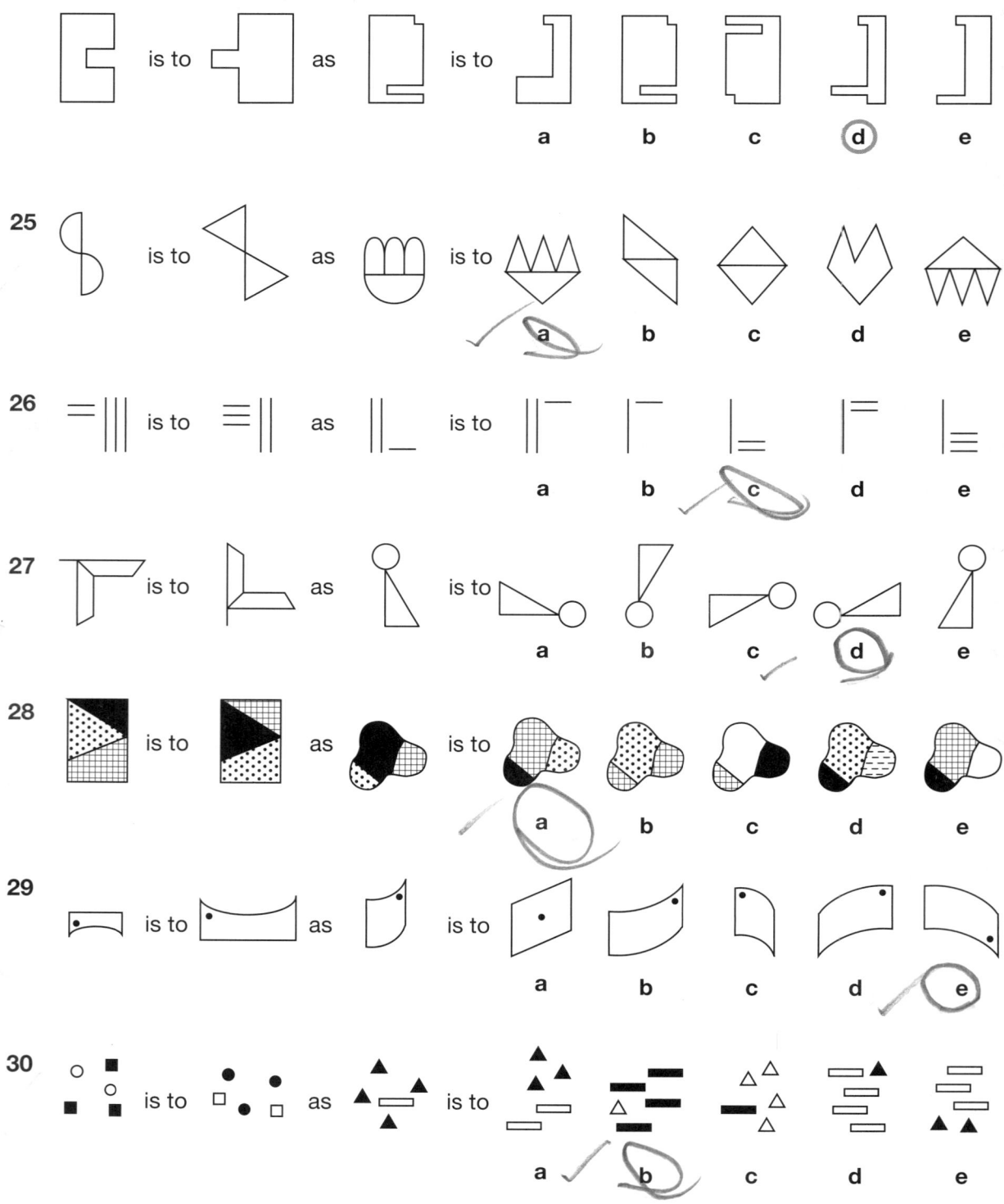

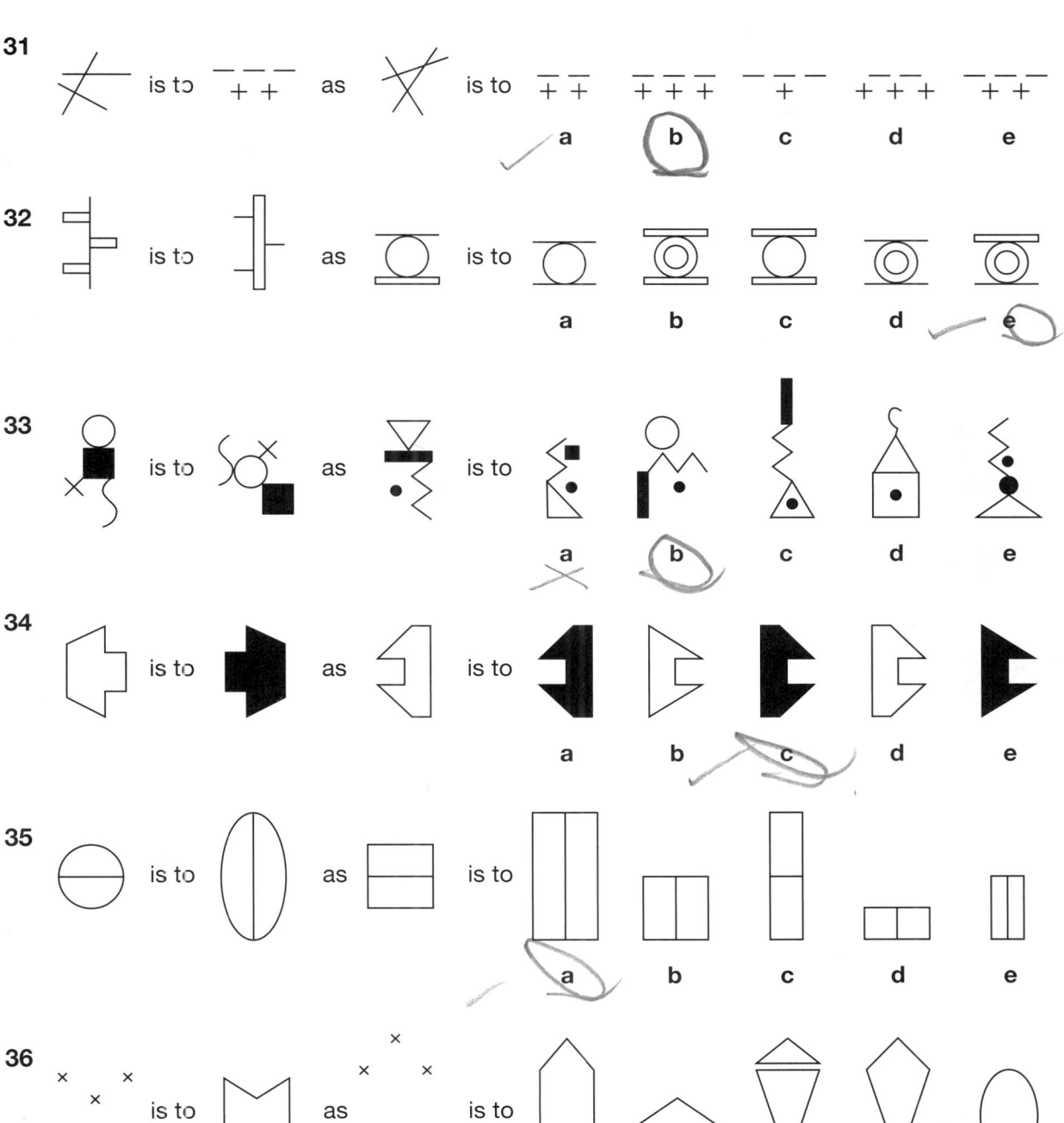

B 6 Which shape or pattern completes the larger square? Circle the letter.

Example

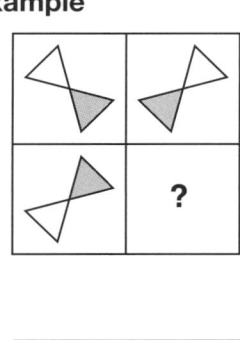 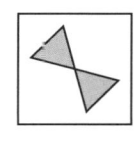 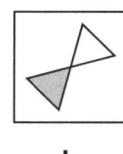 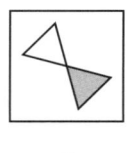 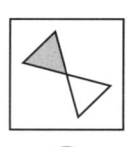 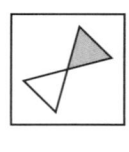

a b c d e

37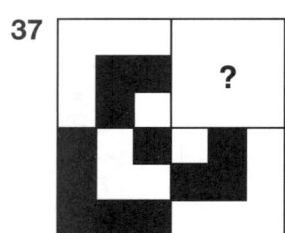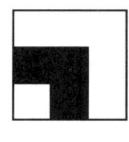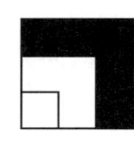

a b c d e

38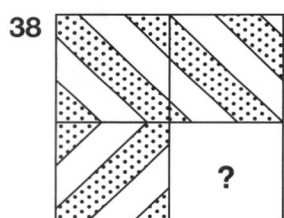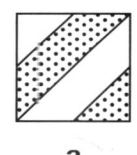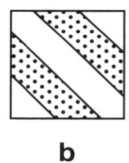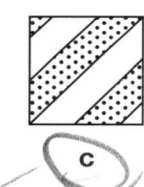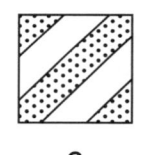

a b c d e

39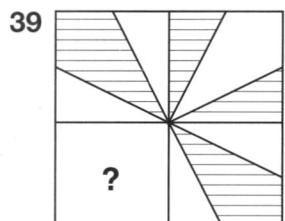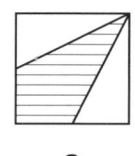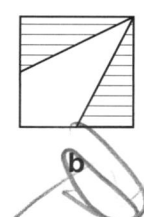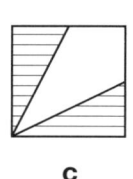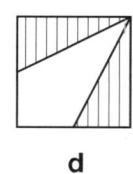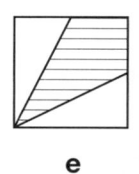

a b c d e

40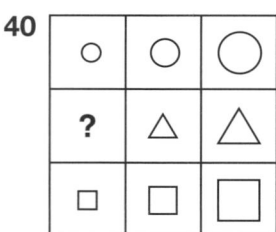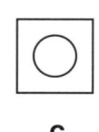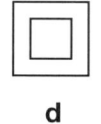

a b c d e

24

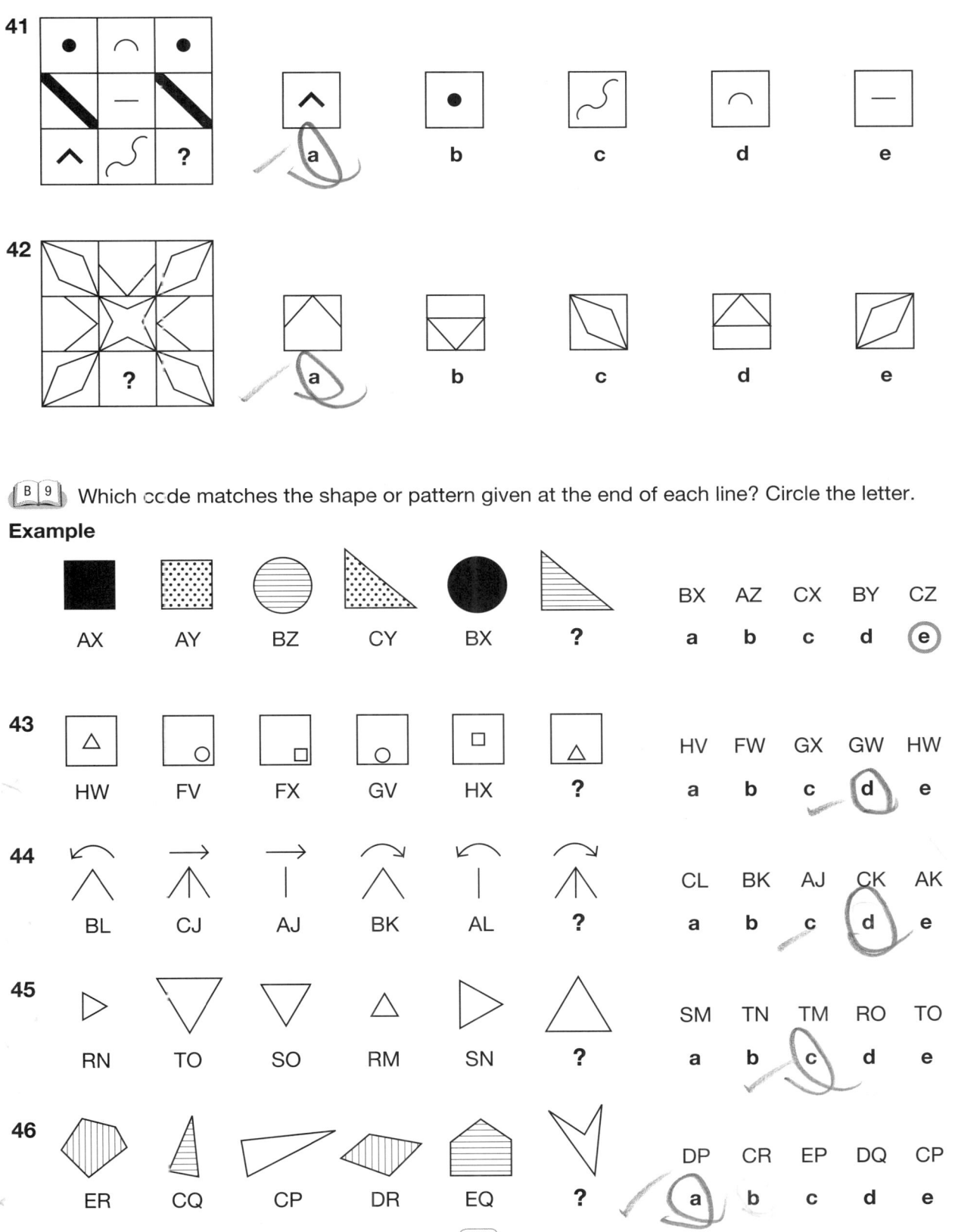

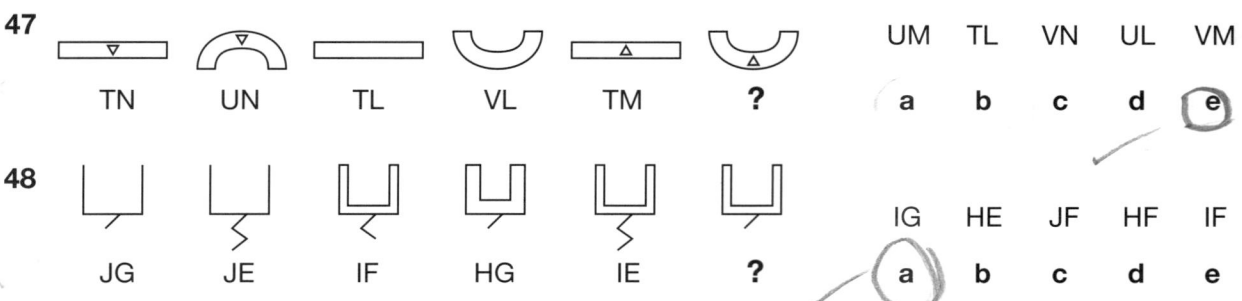

47

TN UN TL VL TM **?**

UM TL VN UL VM

a **b** **c** **d** **e**

48

JG JE IF HG IE **?**

IG HE JF HF IF

a **b** **c** **d** **e**

Which shape or pattern is made when the first two shapes or patterns are put together? Circle the letter.

Example

a **b** **c** **d** **e**

49

a **b** **c** **d** **e**

50

a **b** **c** **d** **e**

51

a **b** **c** **d** **e**

52

a **b** **c** **d** **e**

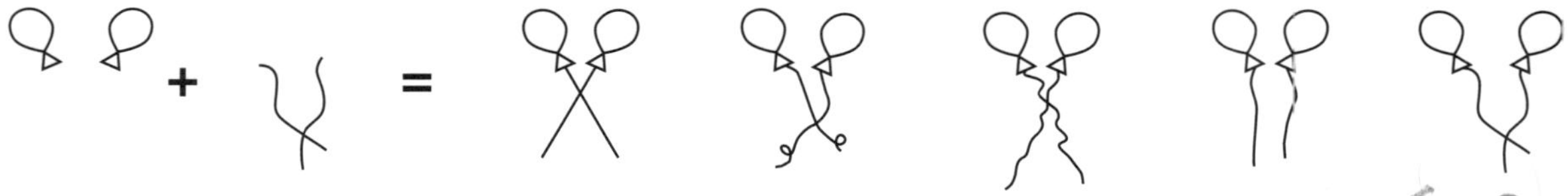

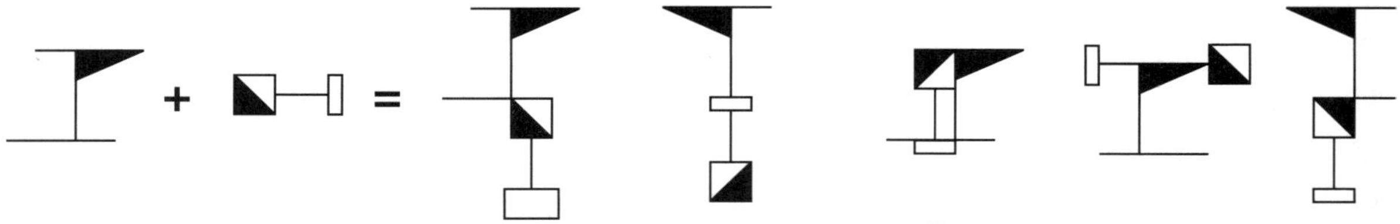

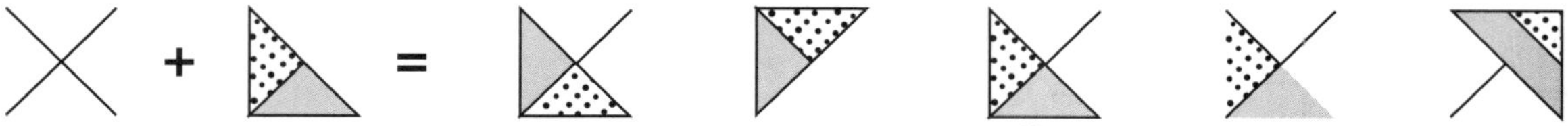

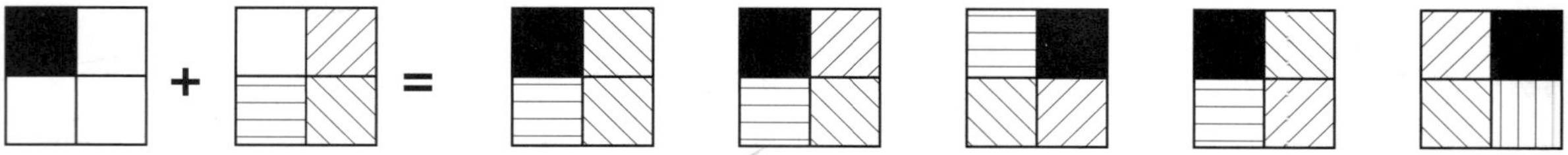

Paper 3

1	d	28	a
2	d	29	e
3	c	30	b
4	a	31	b
5	e	32	e
6	b	33	c
7	c	34	c
8	c	35	a
9	d	36	d
10	a	37	b
11	b	38	c
12	b	39	b
13	e	40	e
14	e	41	a
15	d	42	a
16	c	43	d
17	b	44	d
18	c	45	c
19	a	46	a
20	e	47	e
21	a	48	a
22	d	49	d
23	e	50	e
24	b	51	c
25	a	52	b
26	c	53	c
27	d	54	a

Paper 4

1	d	28	b
2	c	29	c
3	a	30	e
4	e	31	b
5	a	32	c
6	b	33	d
7	b	34	d
8	d	35	e
9	b	36	b
10	e	37	a
11	c	38	d
12	a	39	c
13	b	40	c
14	c	41	d
15	c	42	b
16	d	43	c
17	a	44	b
18	d	45	e
19	c	46	b
20	e	47	c
21	e	48	a
22	b	49	e
23	e	50	b
24	a	51	a
25	a	52	d
26	c	53	e
27	d	54	c

Non-Verbal paper 2

Paper 1

1 c	28 d		
2 b	29 c		
3 e	30 c		
4 b	31 e		
5 a	32 b		
6 e	33 a		
7 d	34 d		
8 e	35 e		
9 c	36 b		
10 c	37 e		
11 a	38 c		
12 d	39 b		
13 b	40 a		
14 e	41 e		
15 e	42 e		
16 a	43 b		
17 c	44 d		
18 b	45 d		
19 c	46 b		
20 d	47 c		
21 a	48 e		
22 b	49 e		
23 d	50 c		
24 a	51 b		
25 b	52 a		
26 e	53 e		
27 b	54 d		

Paper 2

1 c	28 b
2 d	29 e
3 e	30 a
4 c	31 e
5 a	32 d
6 d	33 e
7 d	34 a
8 b	35 c
9 e	36 b
10 a	37 c
11 b	38 e
12 c	39 d
13 b	40 b
14 b	41 e
15 c	42 c
16 d	43 b
17 a	44 e
18 c	45 c
19 d	46 c
20 a	47 c
21 e	48 d
22 b	49 a
23 e	50 b
24 a	51 c
25 d	52 e
26 c	53 d
27 b	54 c

Paper 5

#	Ans	#	Ans
1	a	28	e
2	d	29	b
3	c	30	a
4	b	31	e
5	c	32	c
6	e	33	b
7	e	34	e
8	b	35	d
9	d	36	a
10	a	37	c
11	c	38	c
12	d	39	c
13	a	40	a
14	b	41	d
15	e	42	b
16	d	43	e
17	a	44	e
18	a	45	c
19	e	46	b
20	c	47	e
21	b	48	e
22	b	49	e
23	e	50	d
24	c	51	c
25	b	52	a
26	a	53	c
27	d	54	c

Paper 6

#	Ans	#	Ans
1	e	28	d
2	c	29	e
3	d	30	a
4	a	31	c
5	c	32	b
6	d	33	a
7	e	34	e
8	b	35	e
9	c	36	d
10	a	37	d
11	d	38	c
12	e	39	d
13	b	40	c
14	a	41	b
15	b	42	e
16	e	43	e
17	c	44	a
18	c	45	d
19	b	46	e
20	c	47	c
21	d	48	a
22	a	49	a
23	e	50	d
24	e	51	a
25	d	52	b
26	e	53	b
27	b	54	c

53

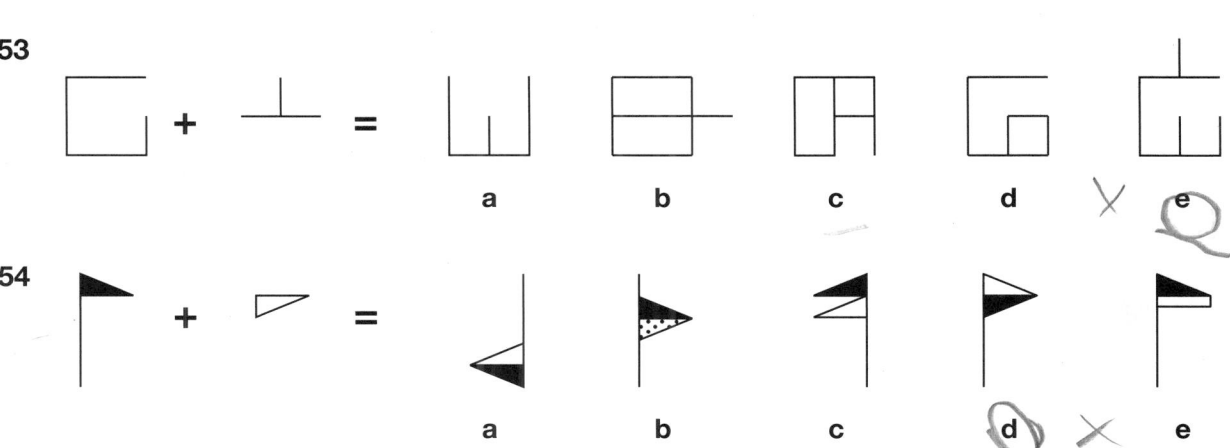

a b c d e

54

a b c d e

Now go to the Progress Chart to record your score! **Total** 54

Paper 4

B 1 Which is the odd one out? Circle the letter.

Example

a **b** **c** **d** **e**

1

a **b** **c** **d** **e**

2

a **b** **c** **d** **e**

3

a **b** **c** **d** **e**

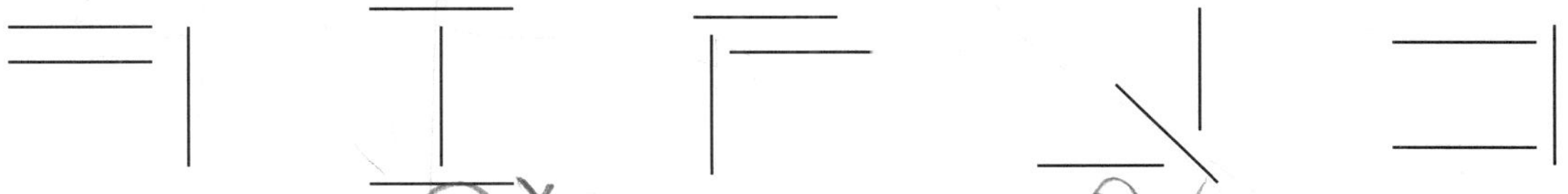

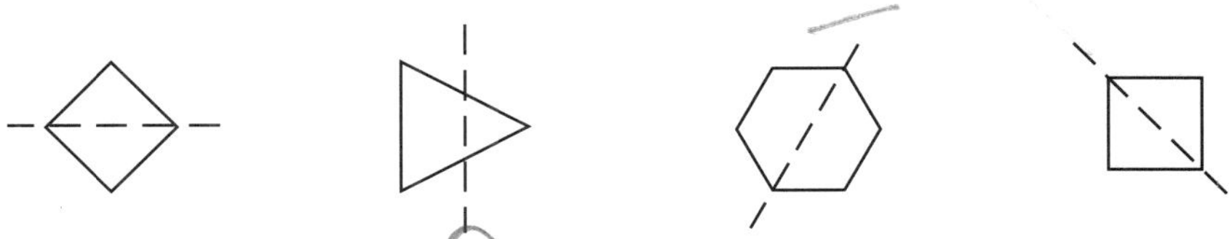

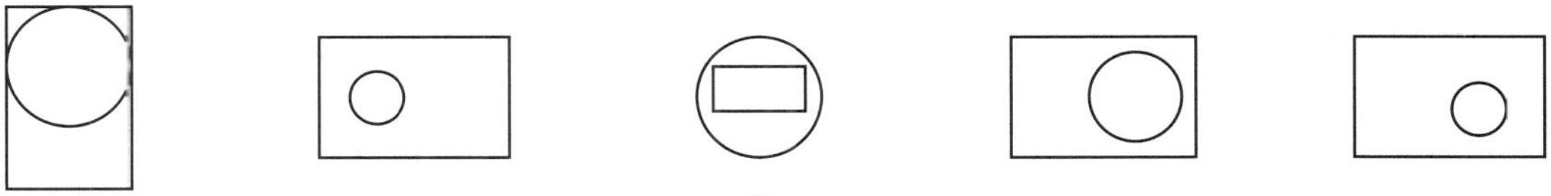

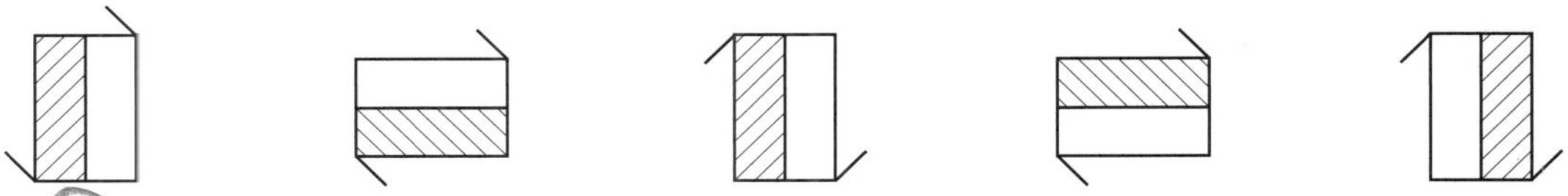

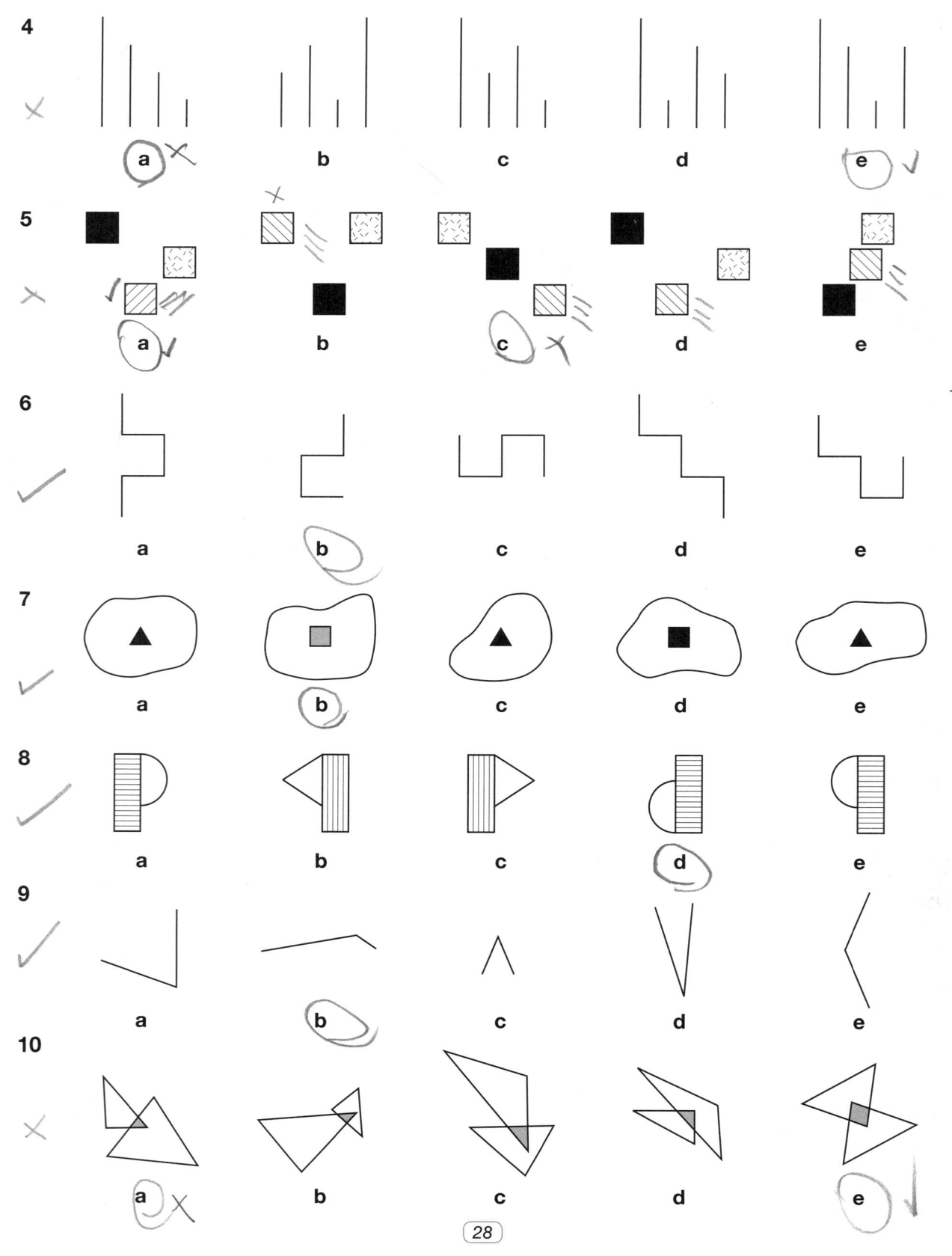

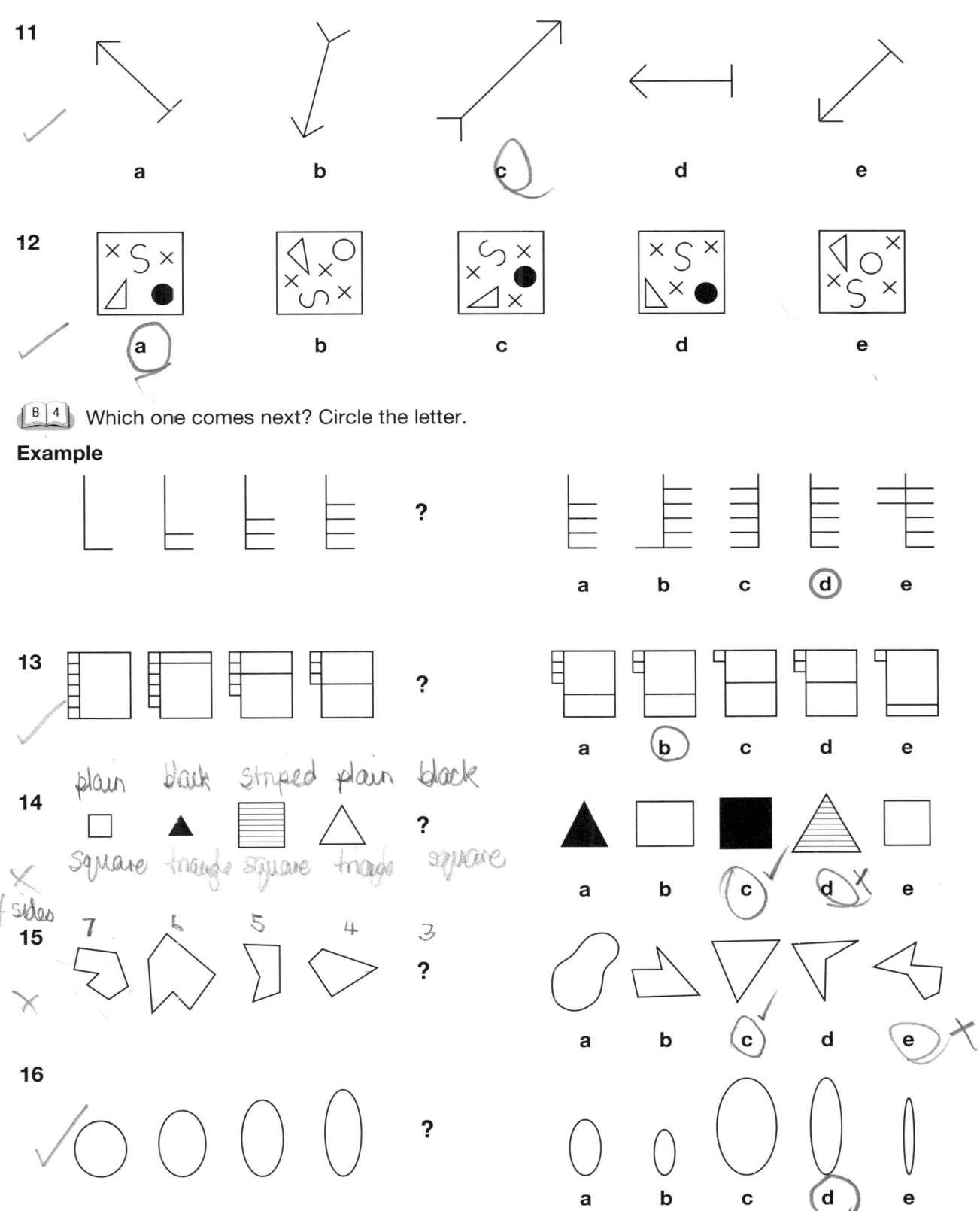

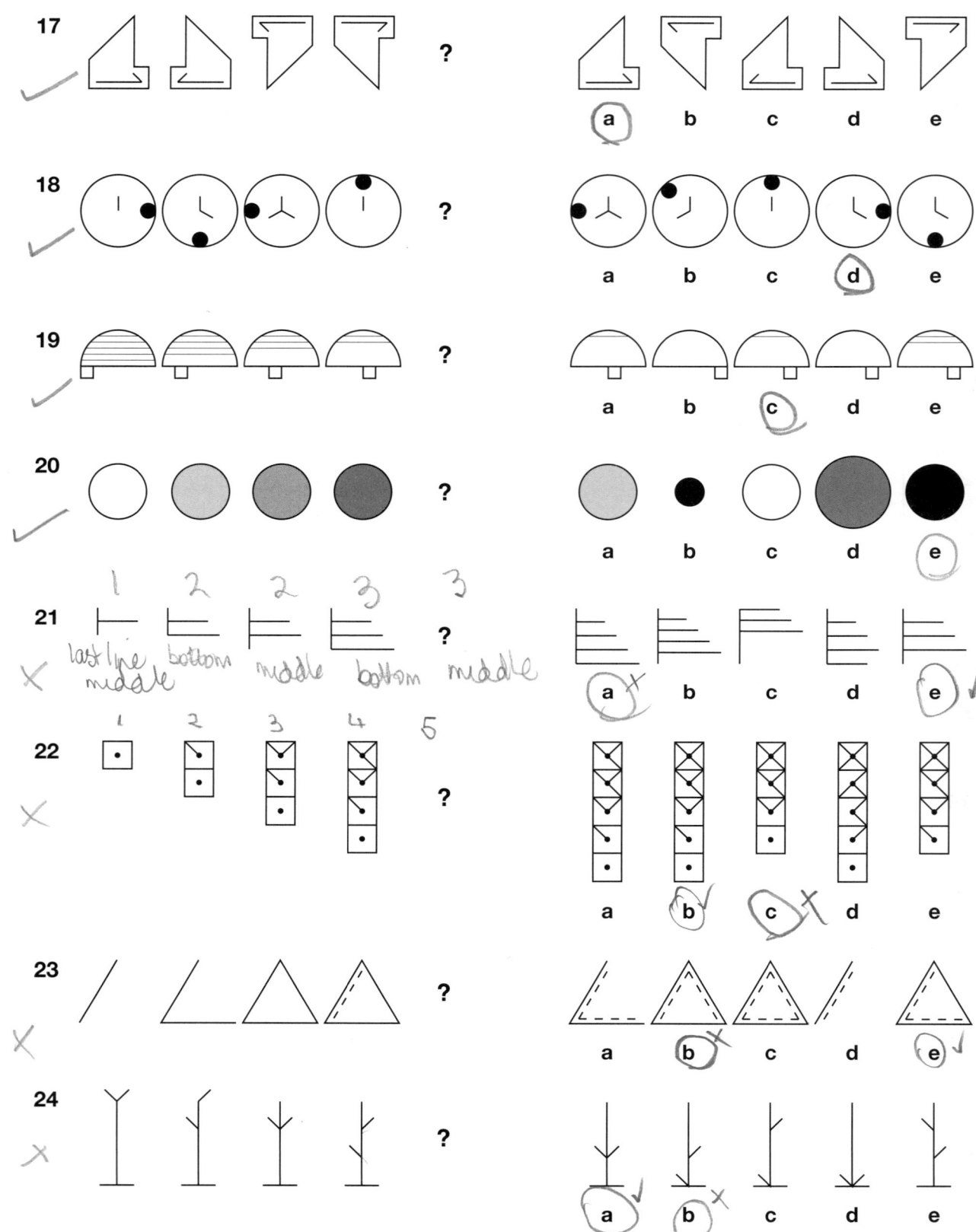

B3 Which shape or pattern on the right completes the second pair in the same way as the first pair? Circle the letter.

Example

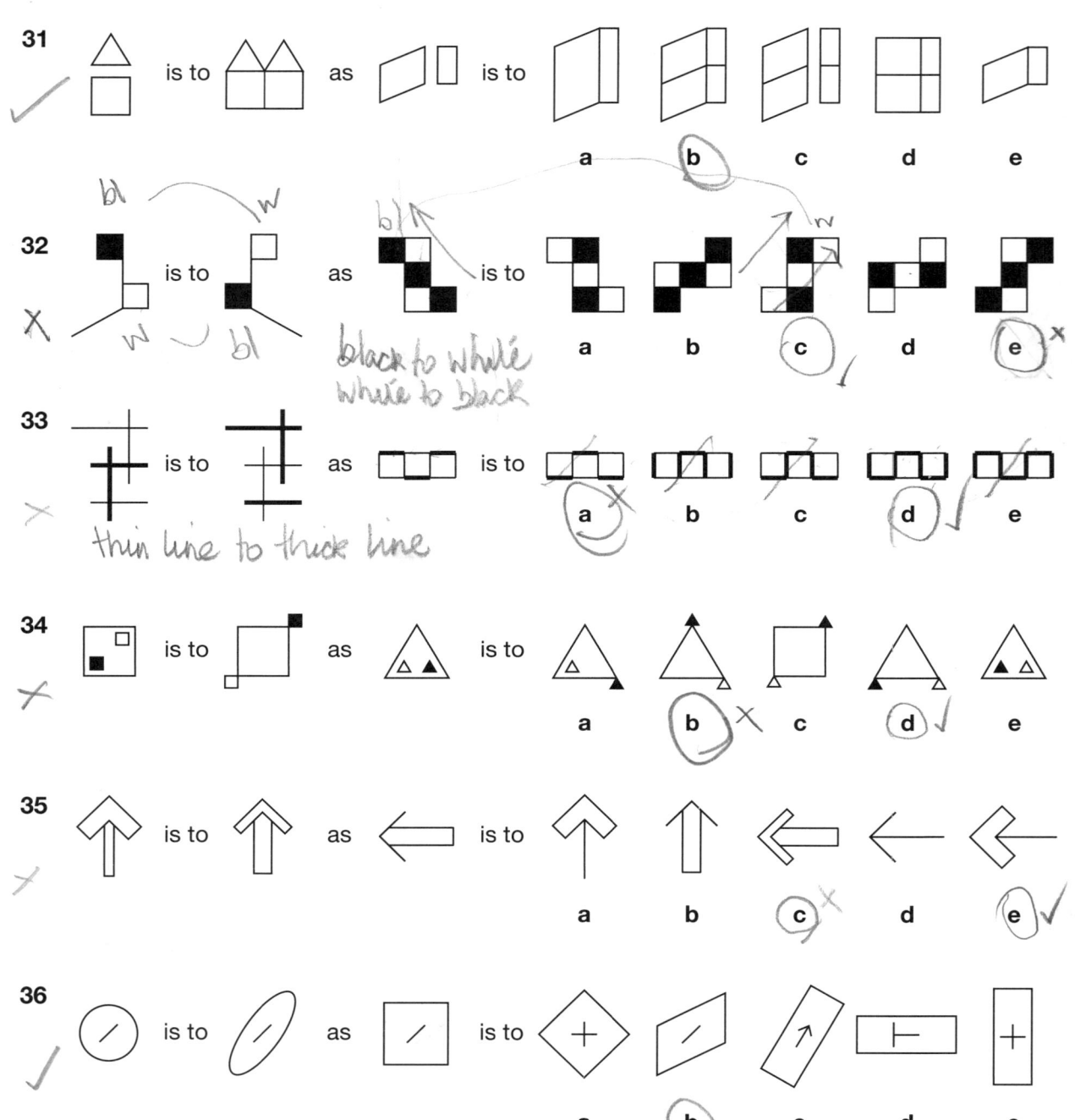

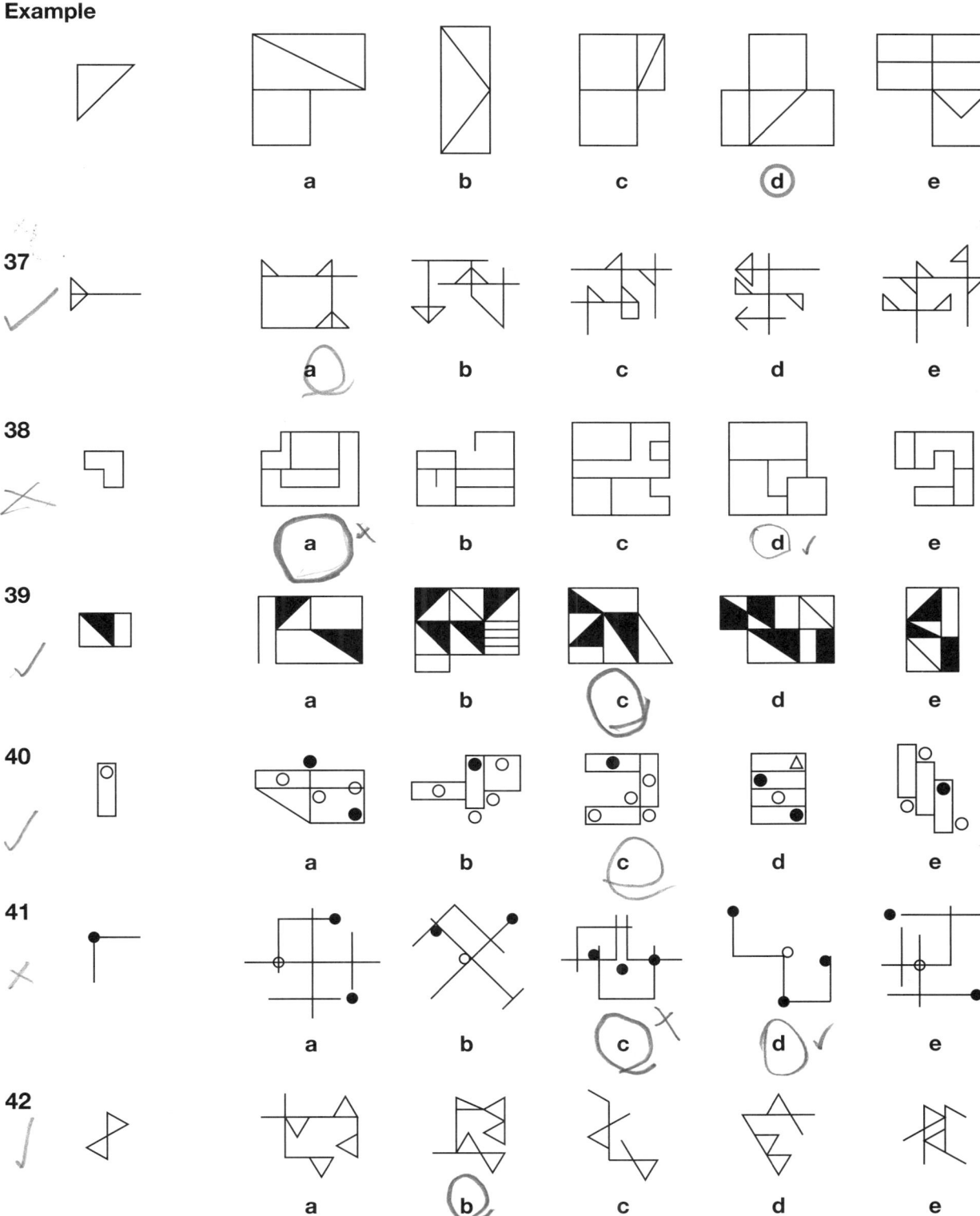

B 6 Which shape or pattern completes the larger square? Circle the letter.

Example

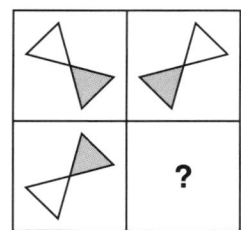 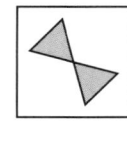 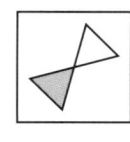 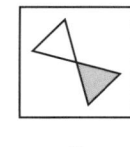 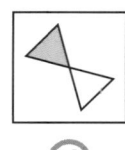 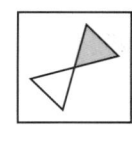
a b c d e

43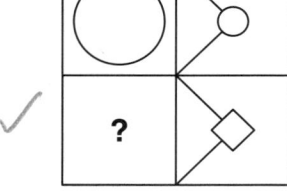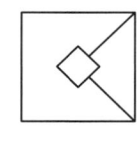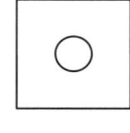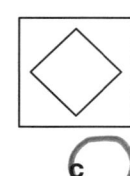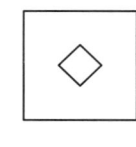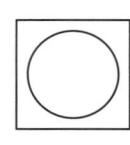
a b c d e

44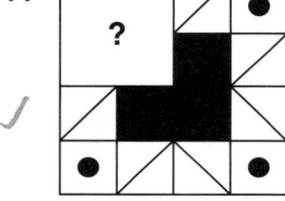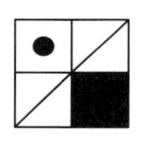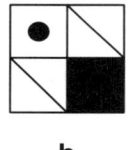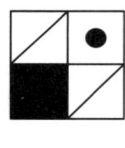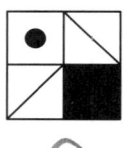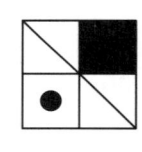
a b c d e

45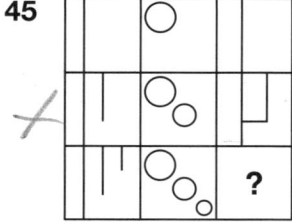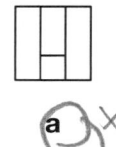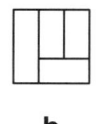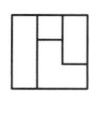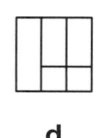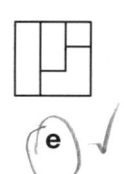
a b c d e

46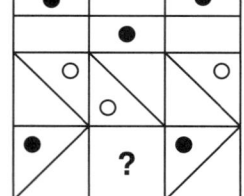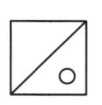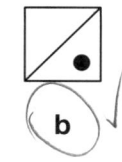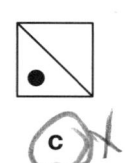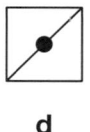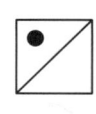
a b c d e

34

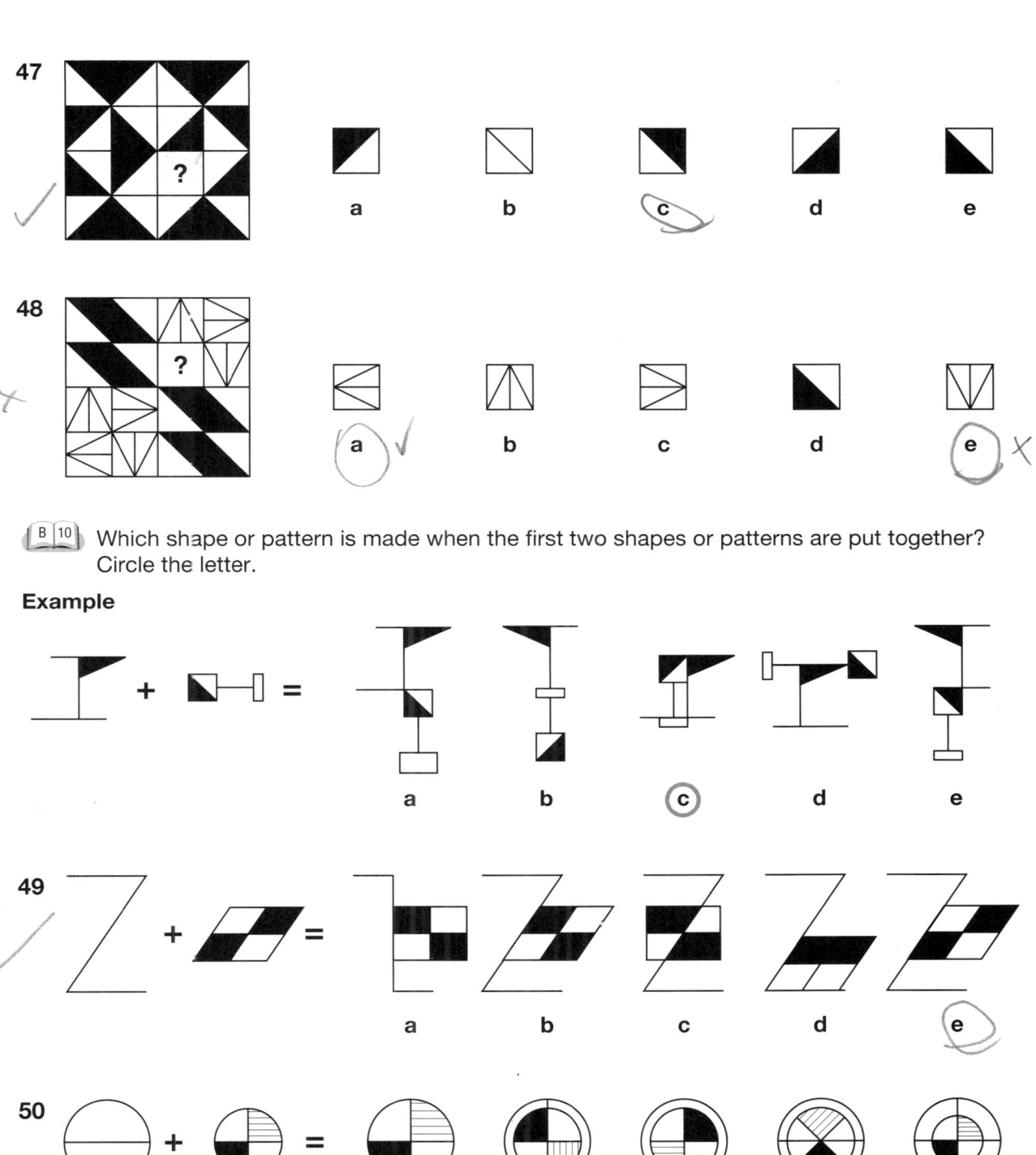

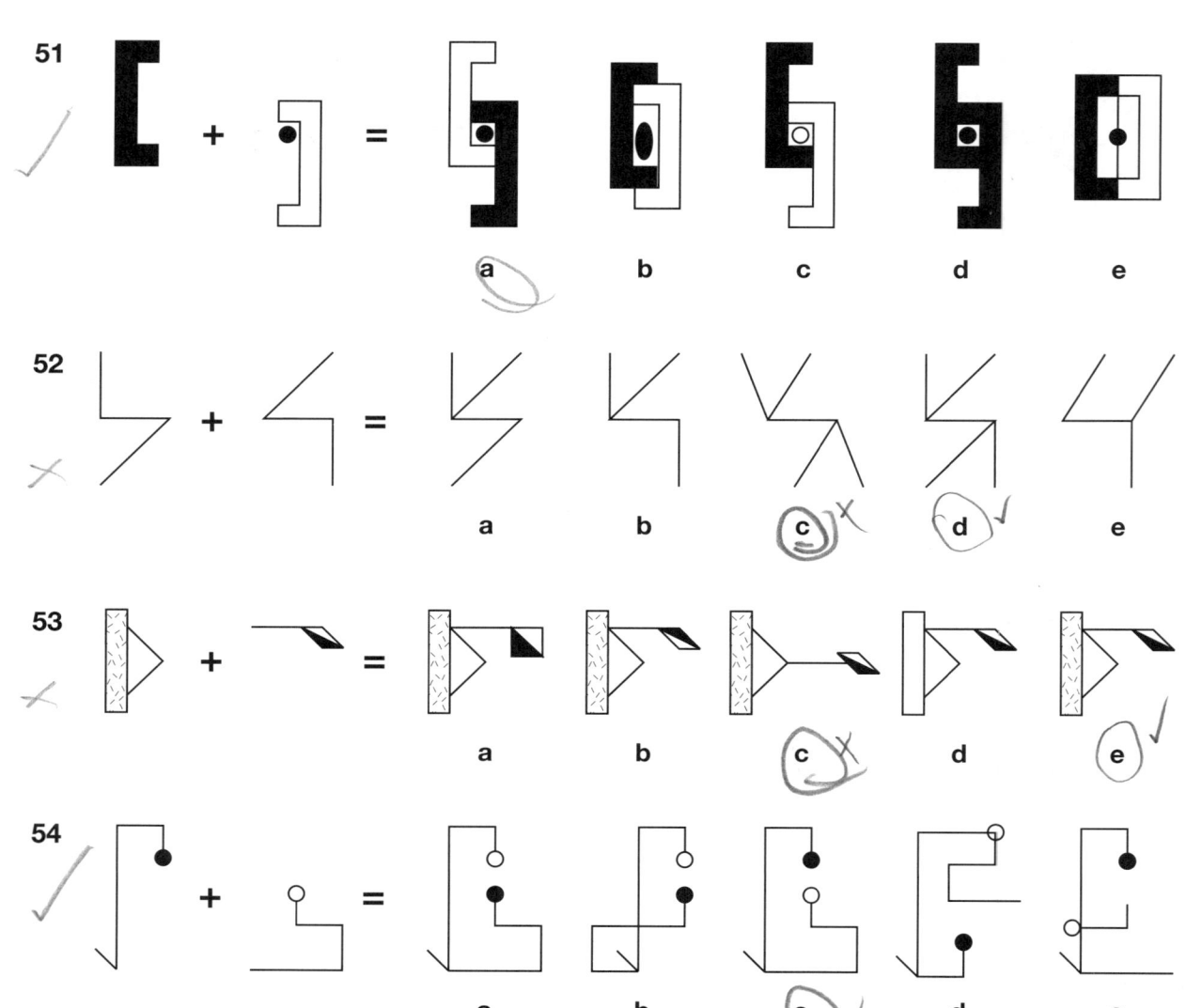

Paper 5

look to these re-do this one

B1 Which is the odd one out? Circle the letter.

Example

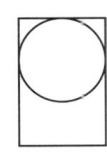 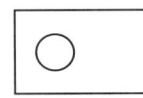 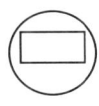 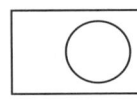 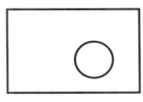
 a   b   c   d   e

1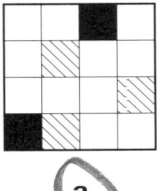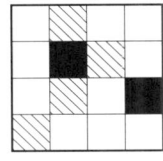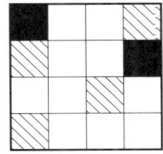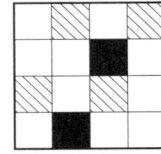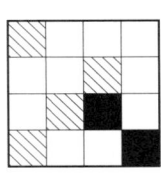
 a   b   c   d   e

2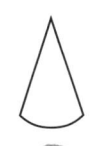
 a   b   c   d   e

3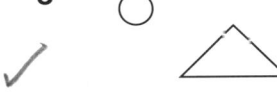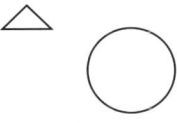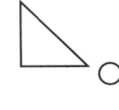
 a   b   c   d   e

4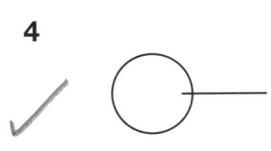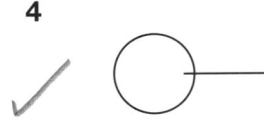
 a   b   c   d   e

5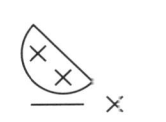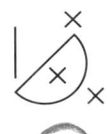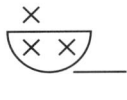
 a   b   c   d   e

37

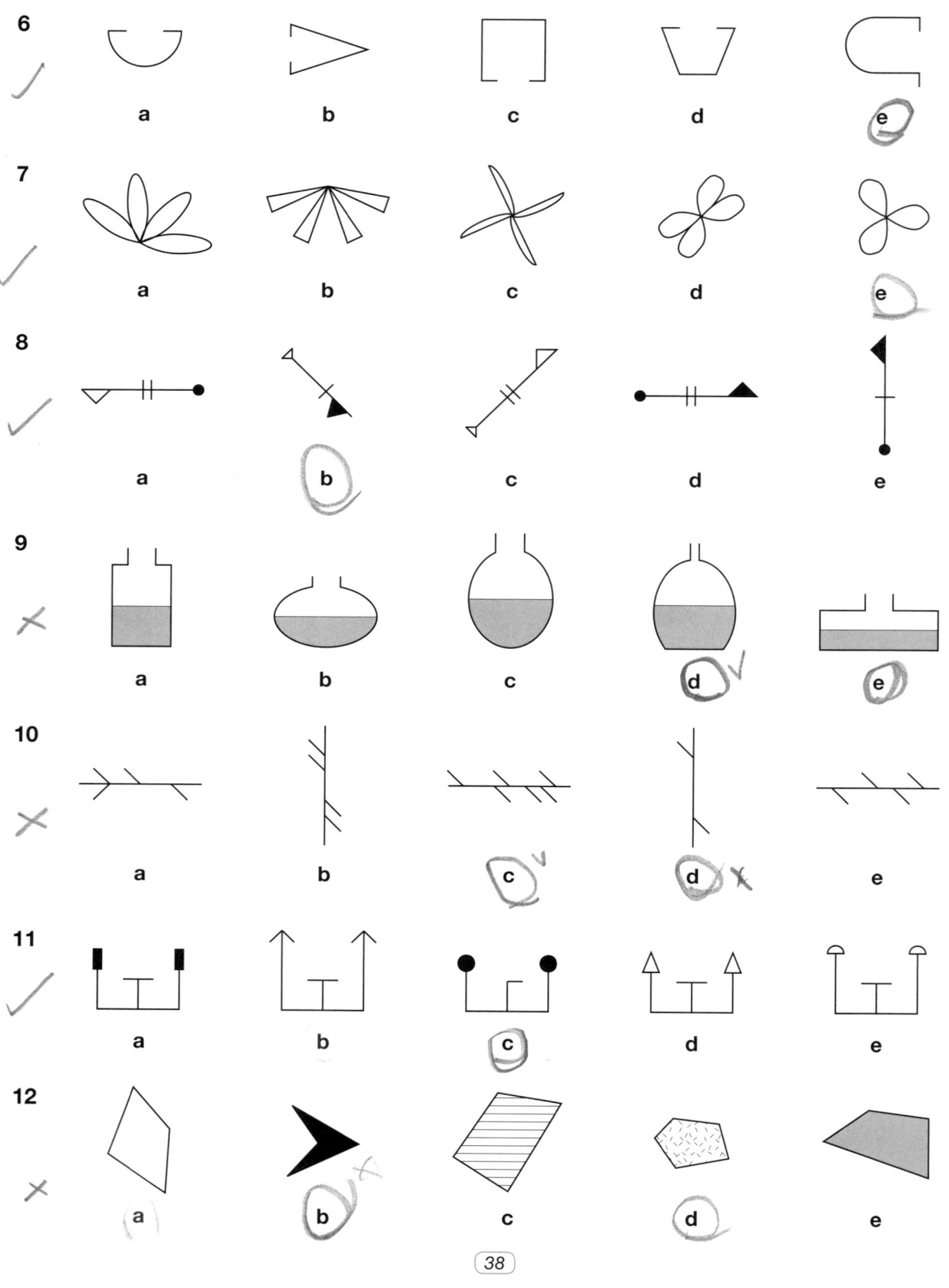

B 4 Which one comes next? Circle the letter.

Example

 ?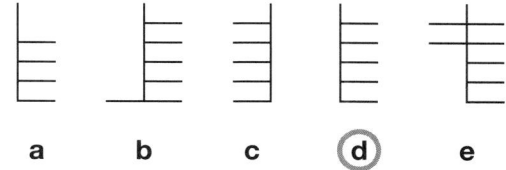

a b c **d** e

13 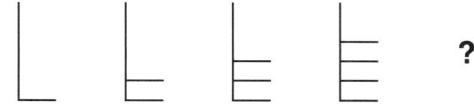 ?

a **b** c d e

14 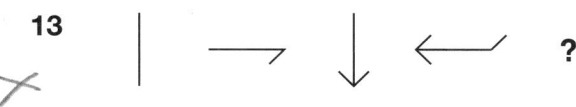 ?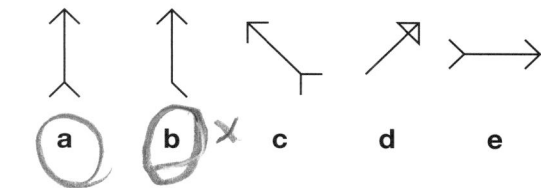

a b c **d** e

15 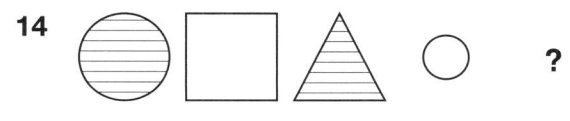 ?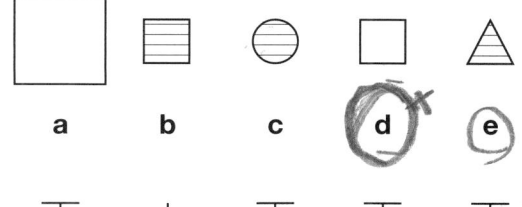

a b c d **e**

16  ?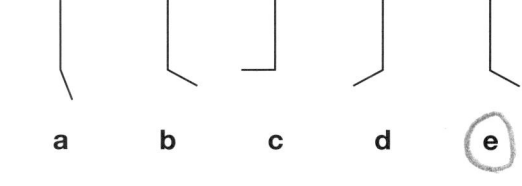

a b c **d** e

17 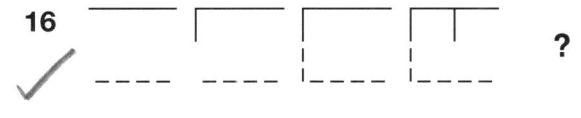 ?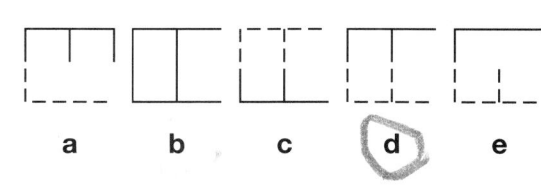

a **b** c d **e**

18 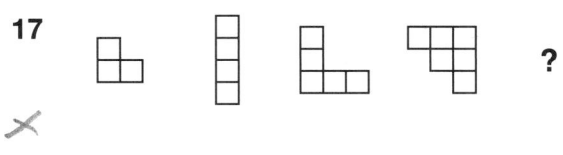 ?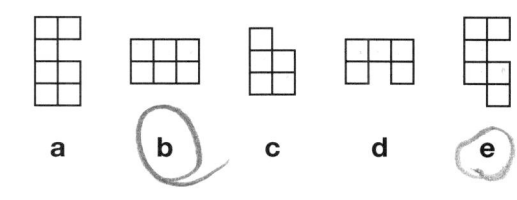

a b c d e

39

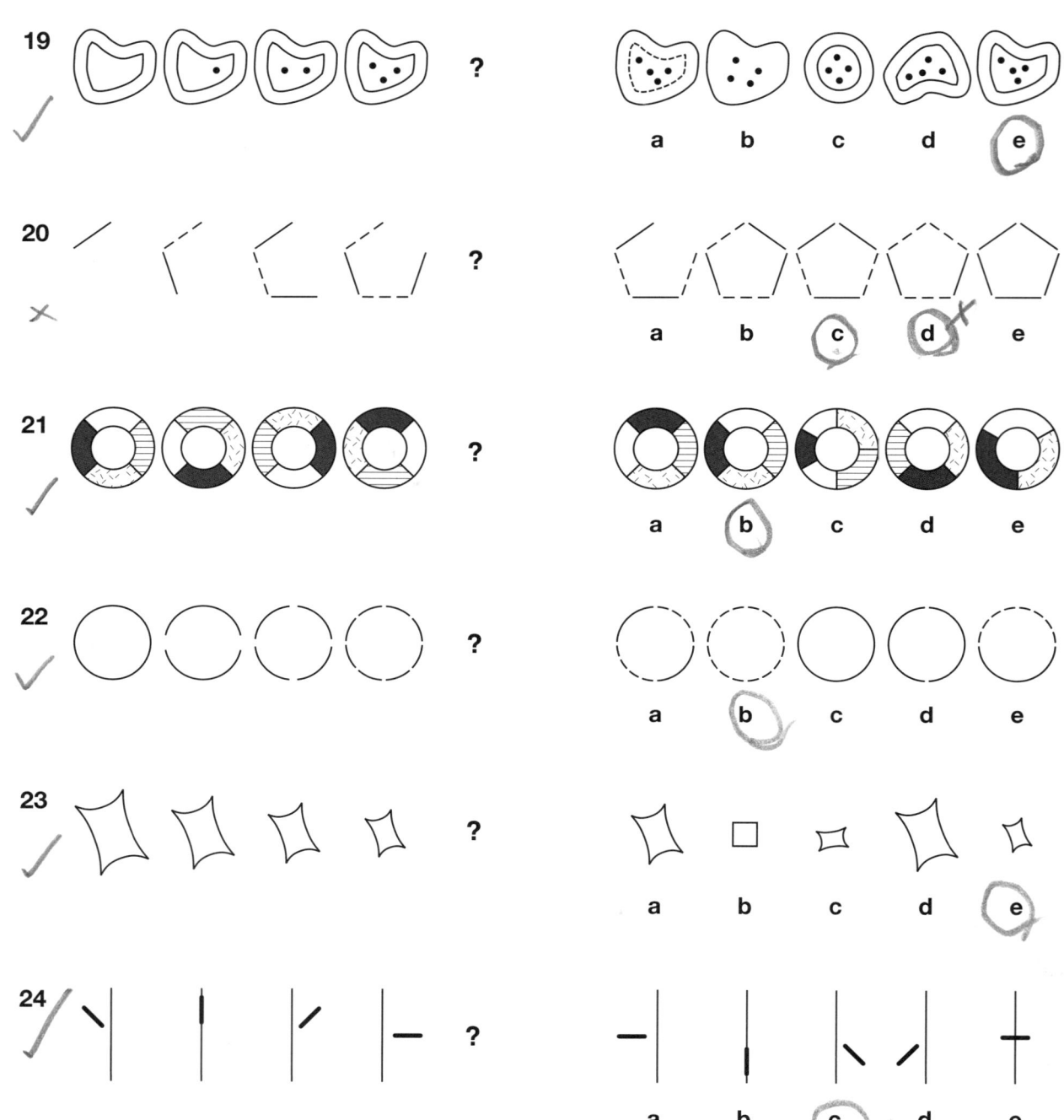

B3 Which shape or pattern on the right completes the second pair in the same way as the first pair? Circle the letter.

Example

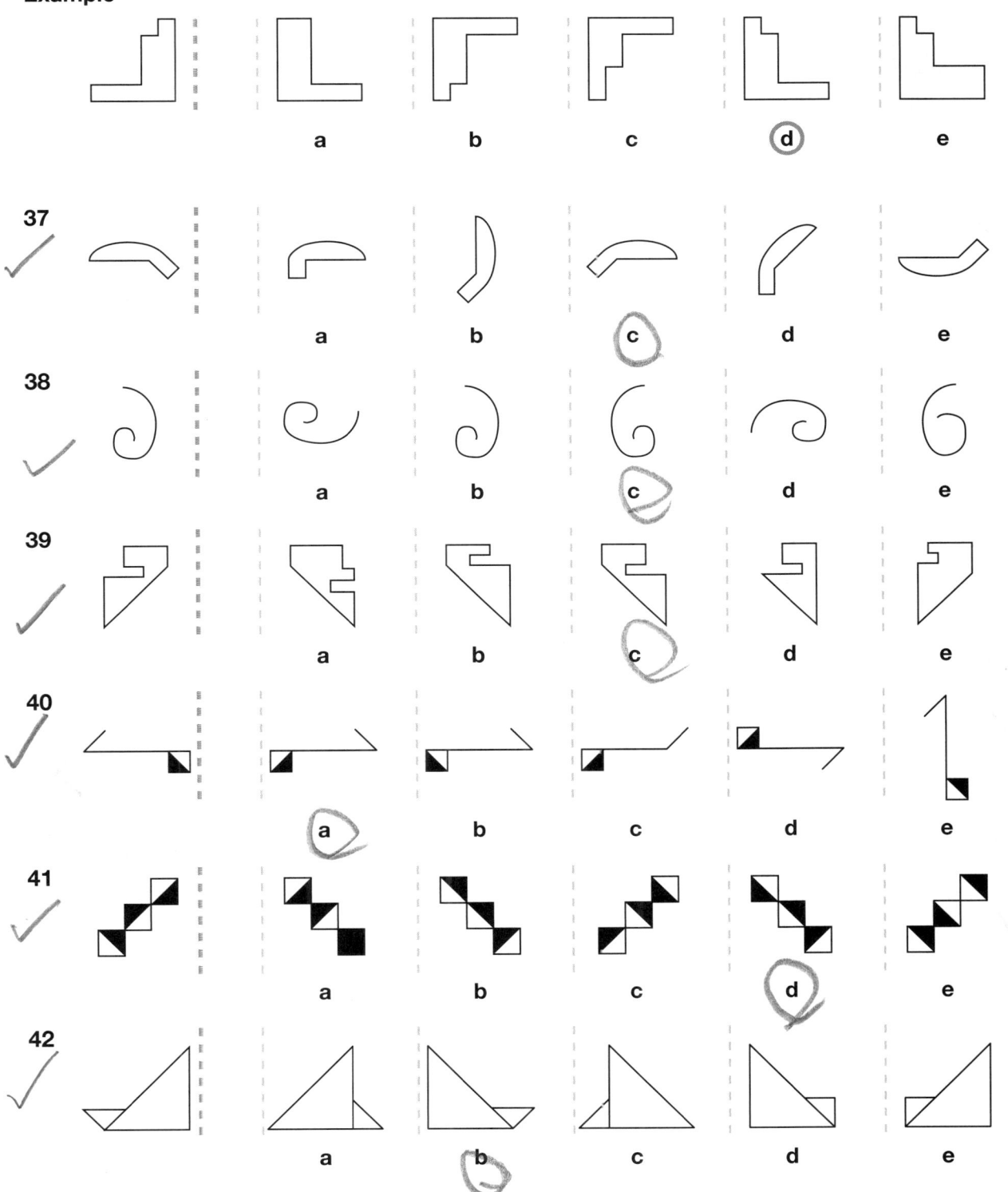

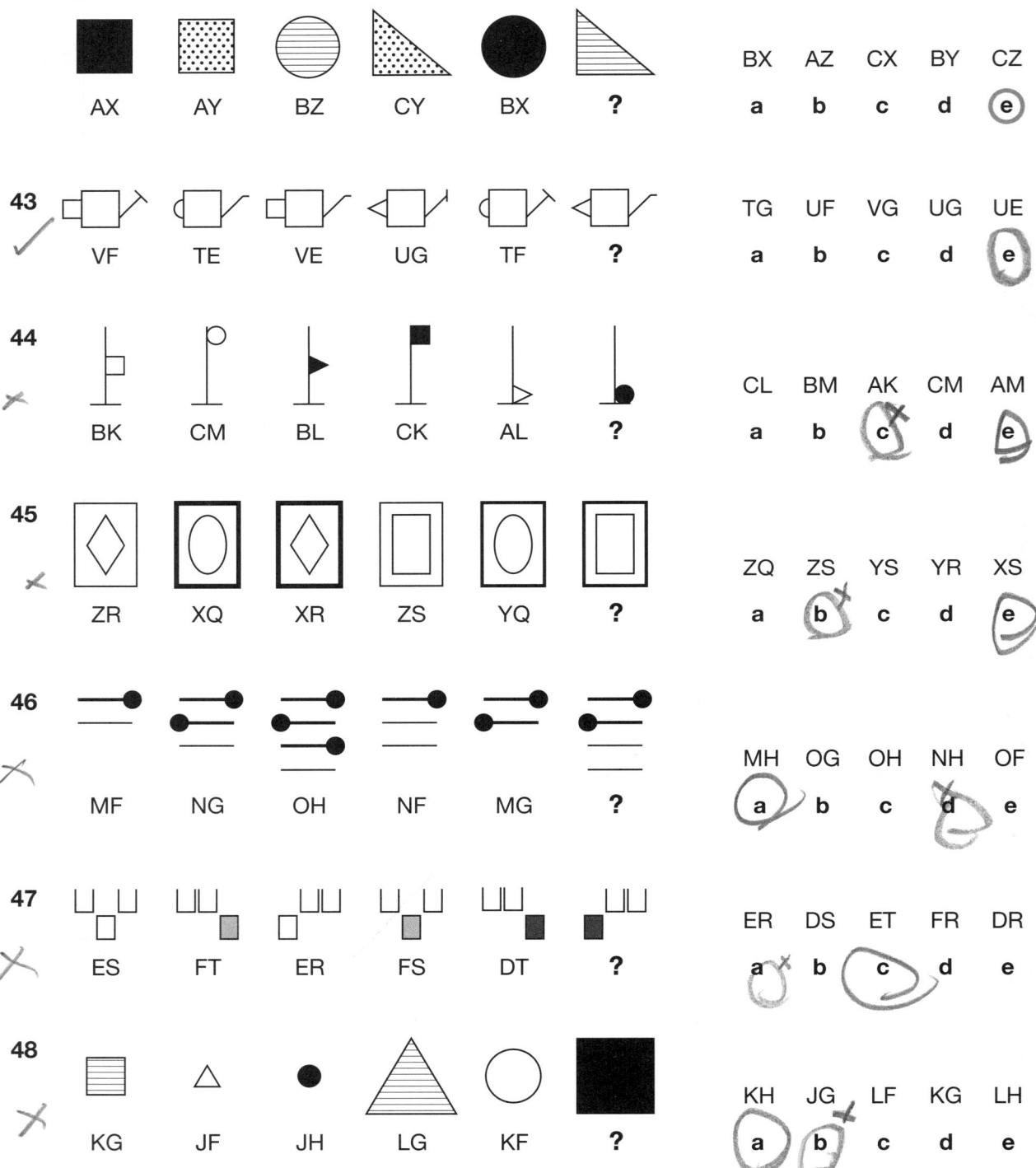

B 8 Which cube cannot be made from the given net? Circle the letter.

Example

 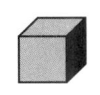

a b c (d) e

49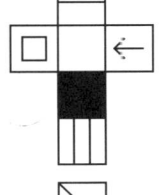

a b c d e

50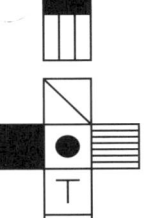

a b c d e

51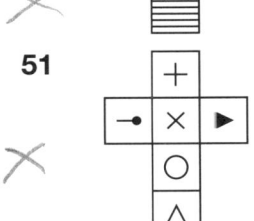

a b c d e

52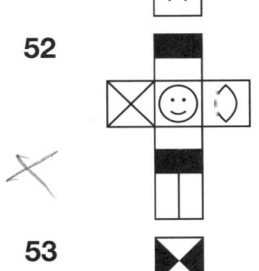

a b c d e

53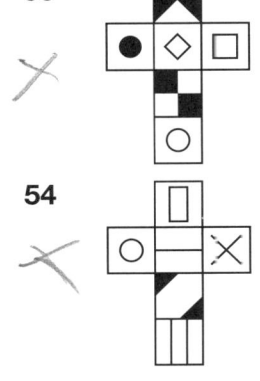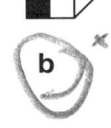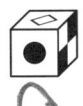

a b c d e

54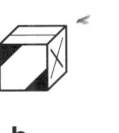

a b c d e

Now go to the Progress Chart ... 45 ... to record your score! Total 33 54

Paper 6

14th Aug

B1 Which is the odd one out? Circle the letter.

Example

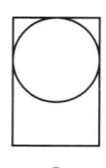 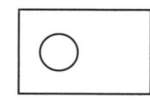 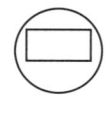 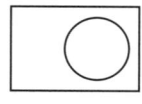 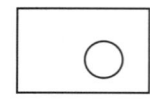
   a   b   ⓒ   d   e

1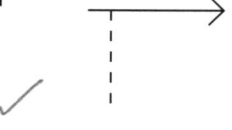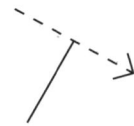
   a   b   c   d   e

2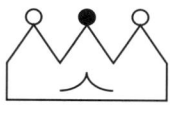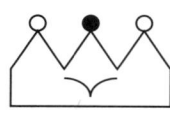
   a   b   c   d   e

3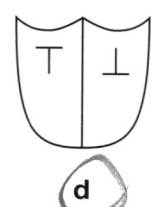
   a   b   c   d   e

4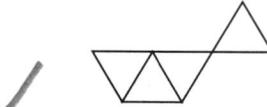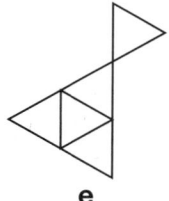
   a   b   c   d   e

5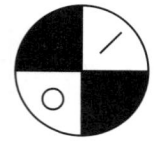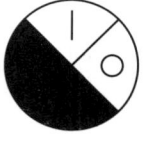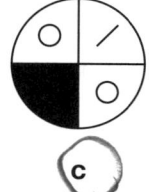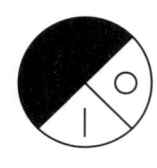
   a   b   c   d   e

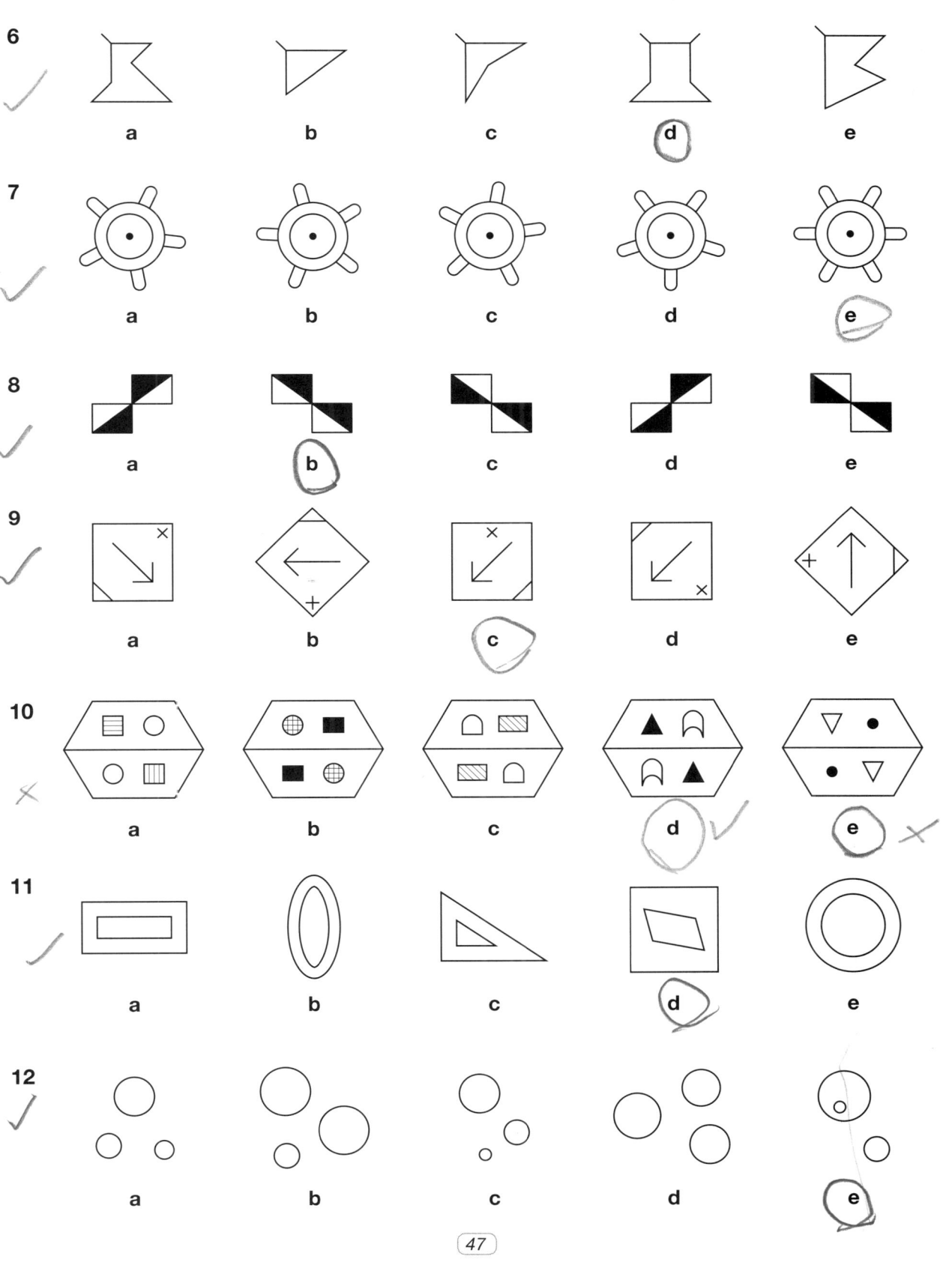

B 4 Which one comes next? Circle the letter.

Example

 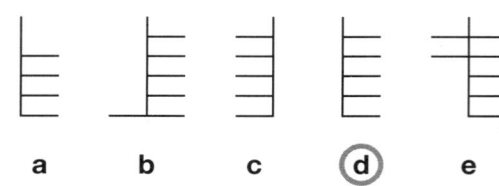

a b c (d) e

13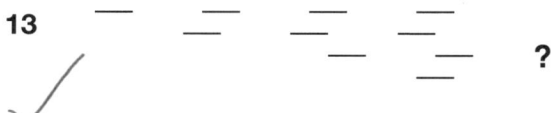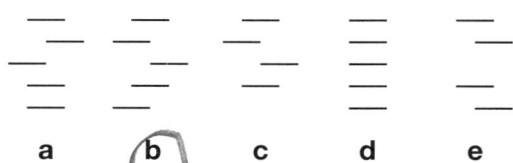

a (b) c d e

14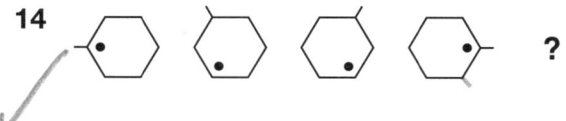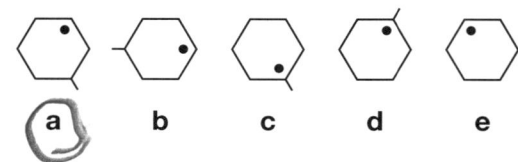

(a) b c d e

15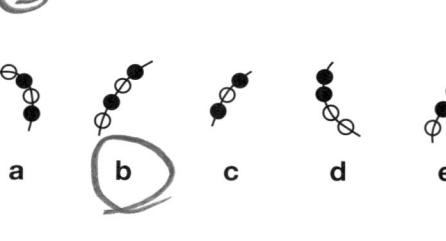

a (b) c d e

16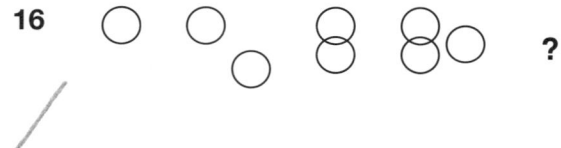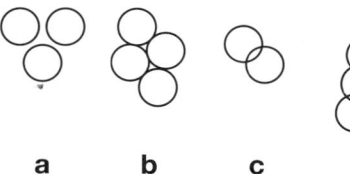

a b c d (e)

17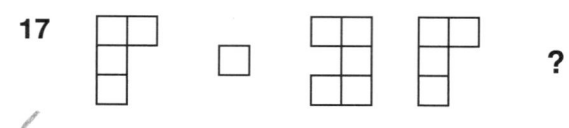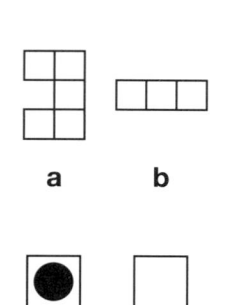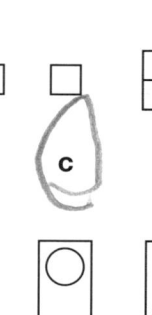

a b (c) d e

18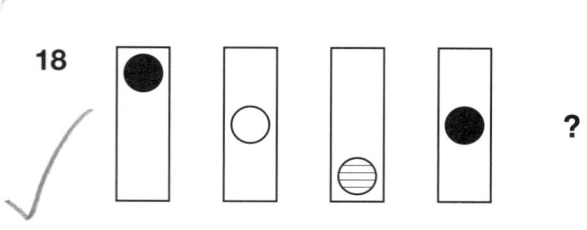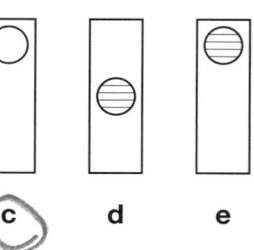

a b (c) d e

48

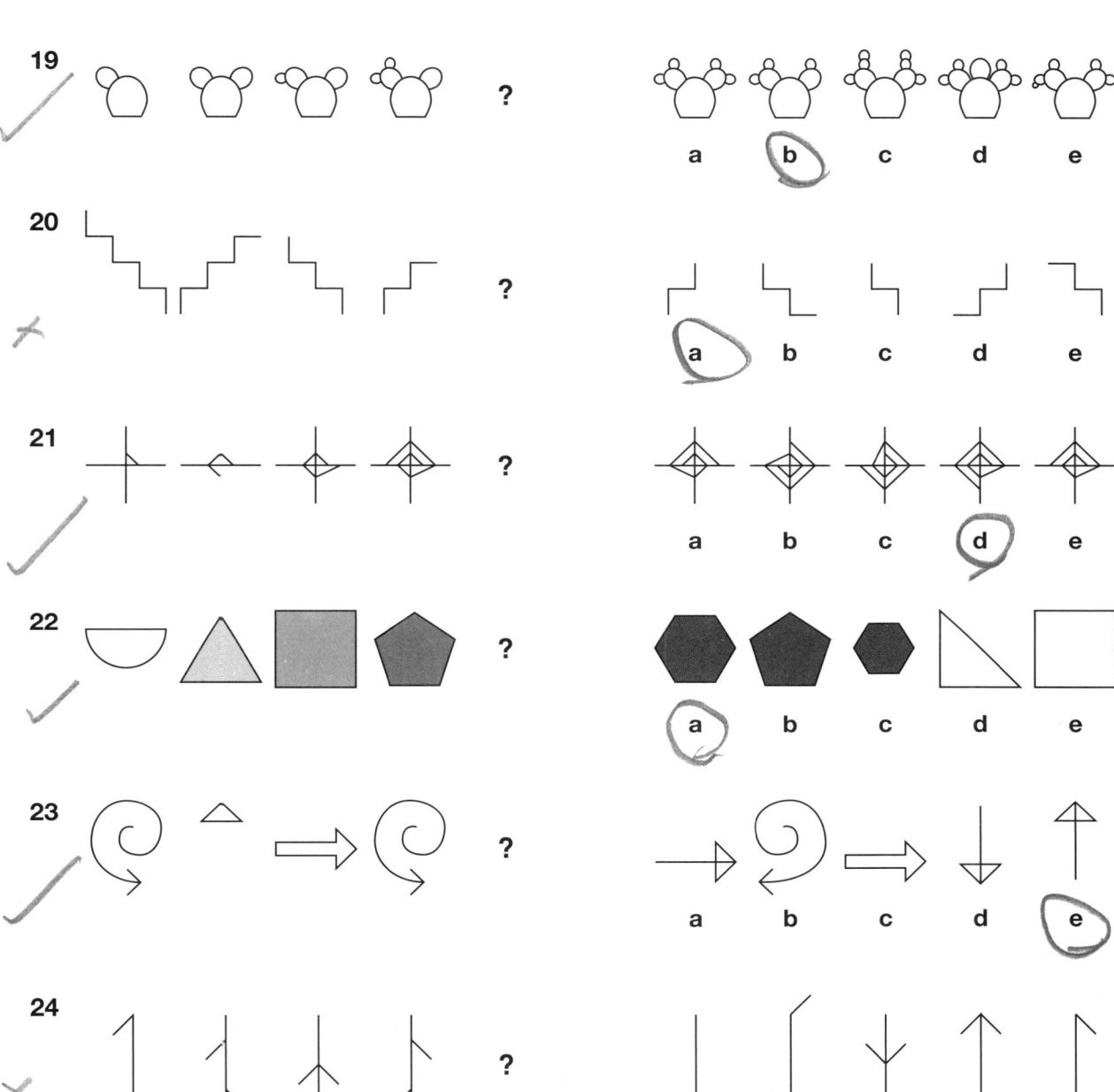

B3 Which shape or pattern on the right completes the second pair in the same way as the first pair? Circle the letter.

Example

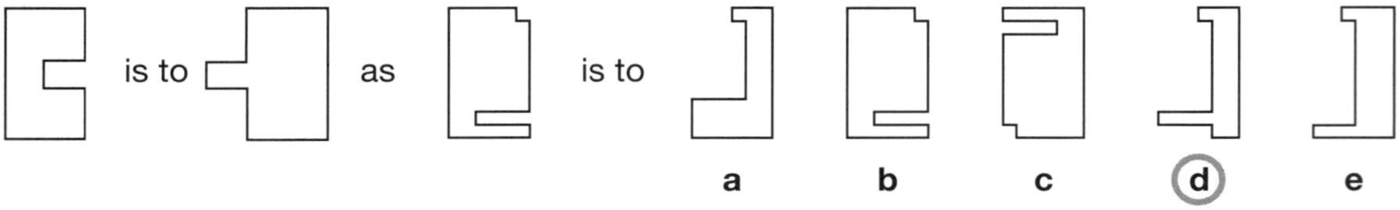

25

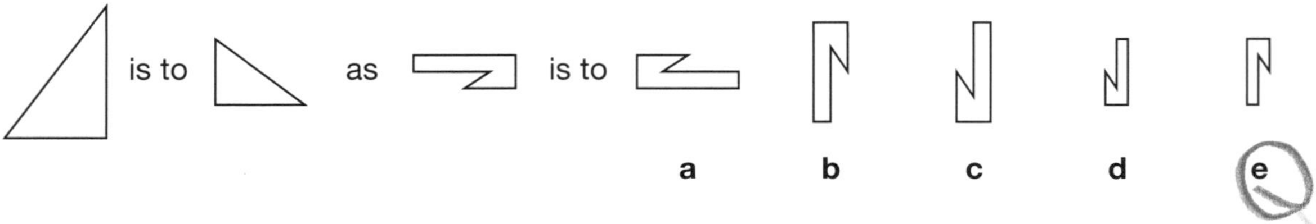

26

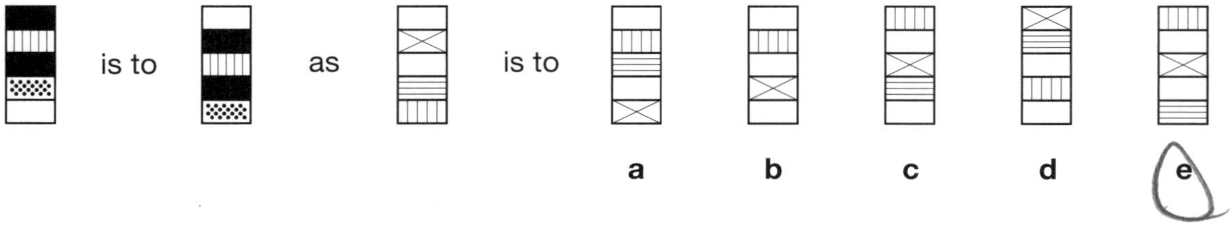

27

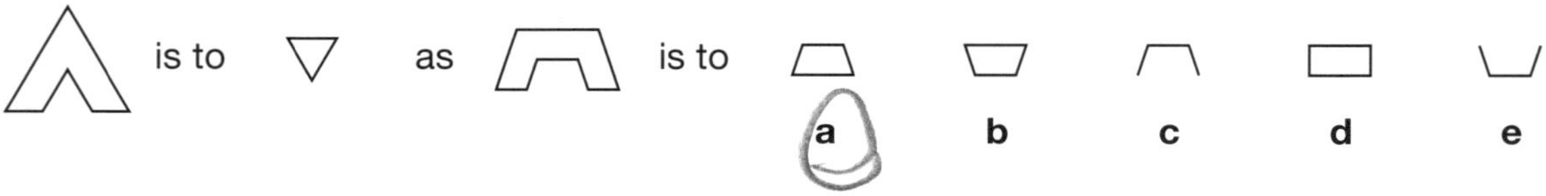

28

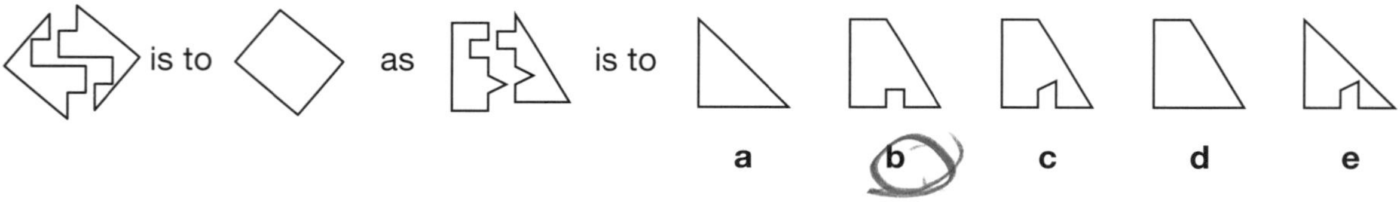

29

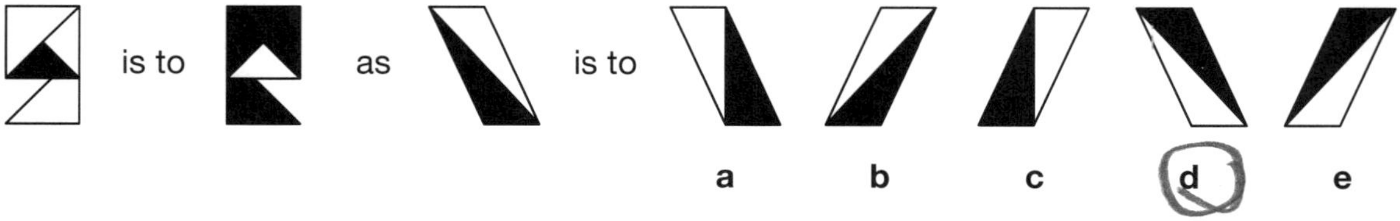

30

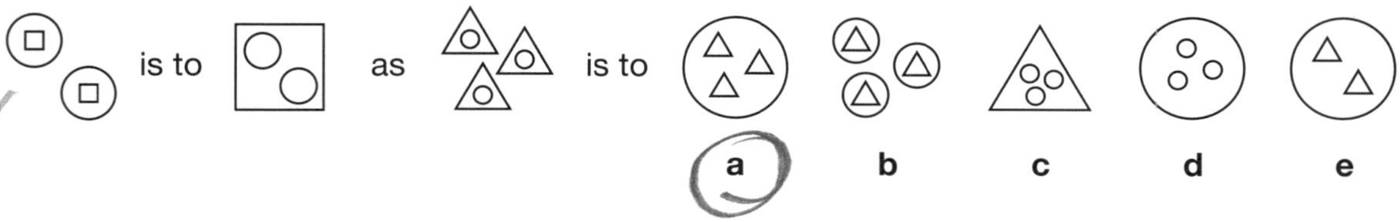

50

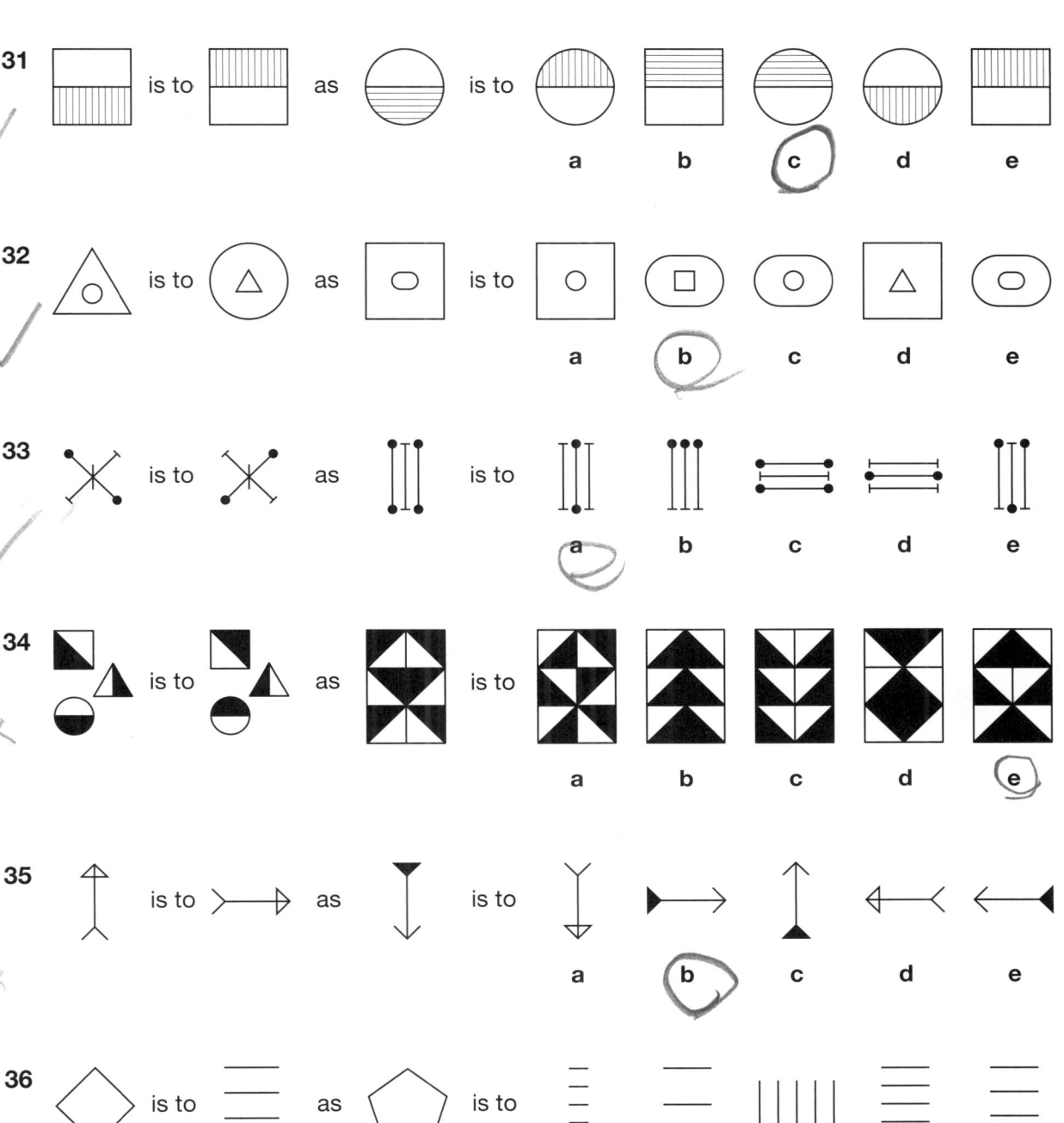

B6 Which shape or pattern completes the larger square? Circle the letter.

Example

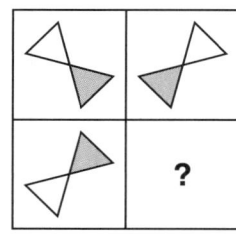 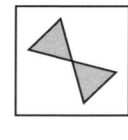 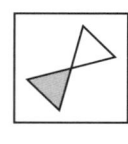 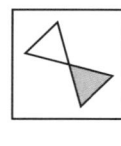 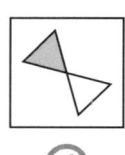 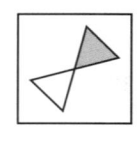
a b c (d) e

37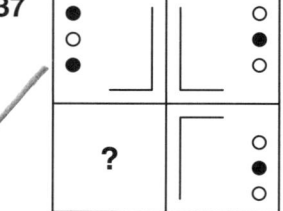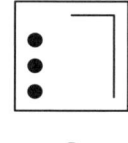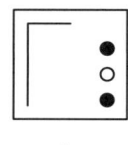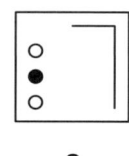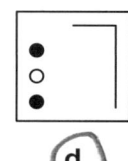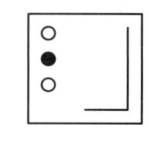
a b c (d) e

38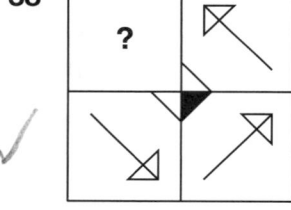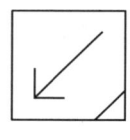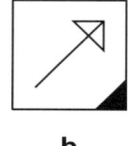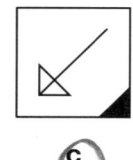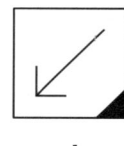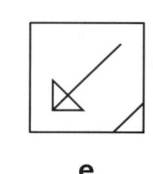
a b (c) d e

39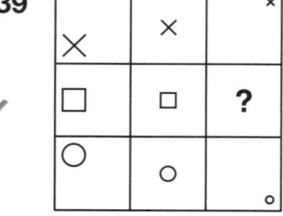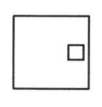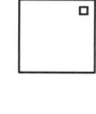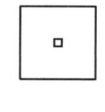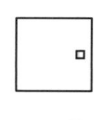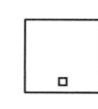
a b c (d) e

40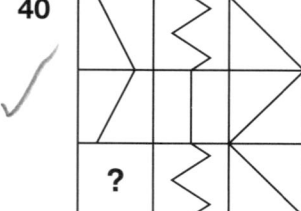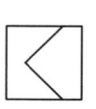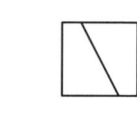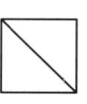
a b (c) d e

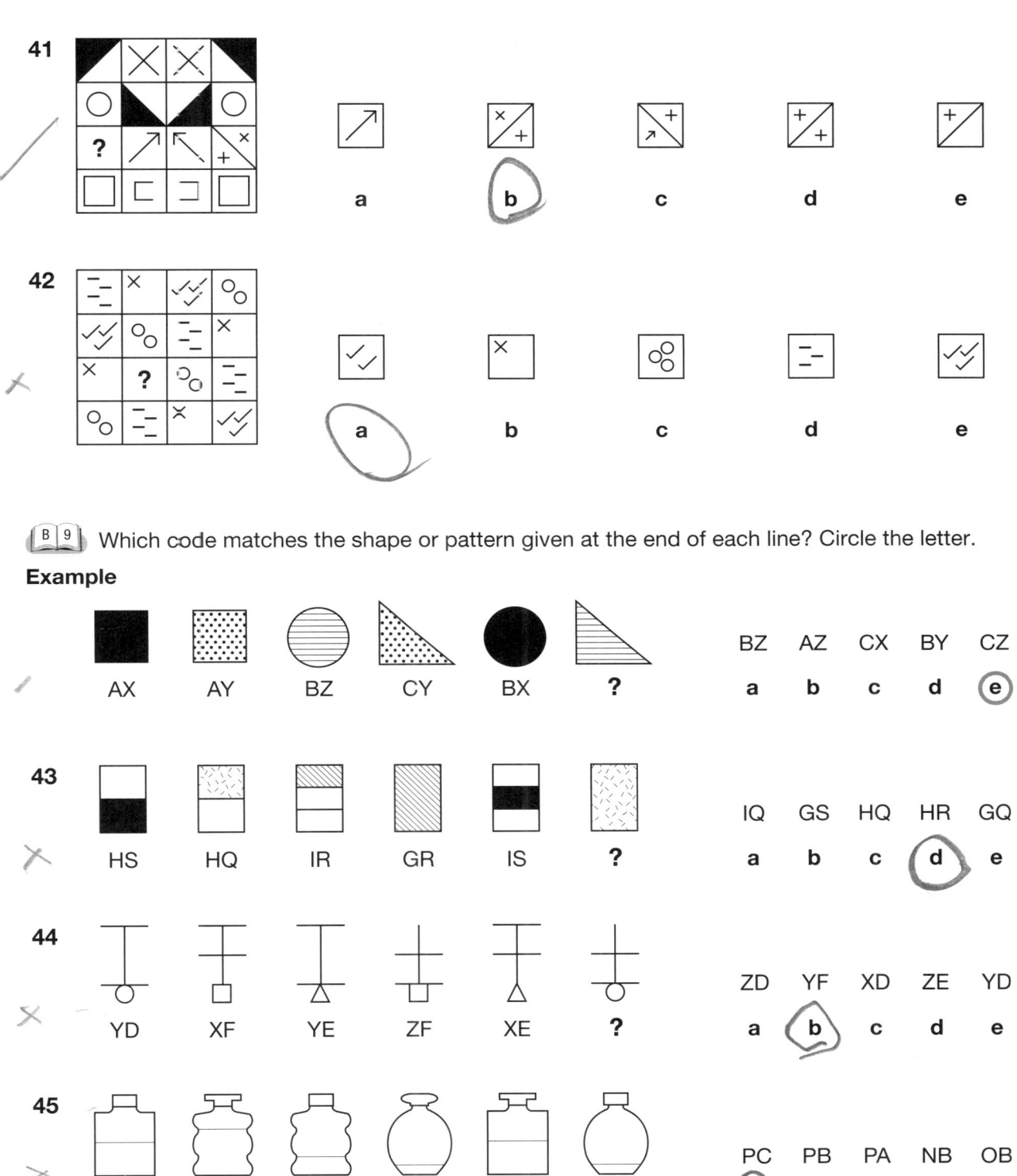

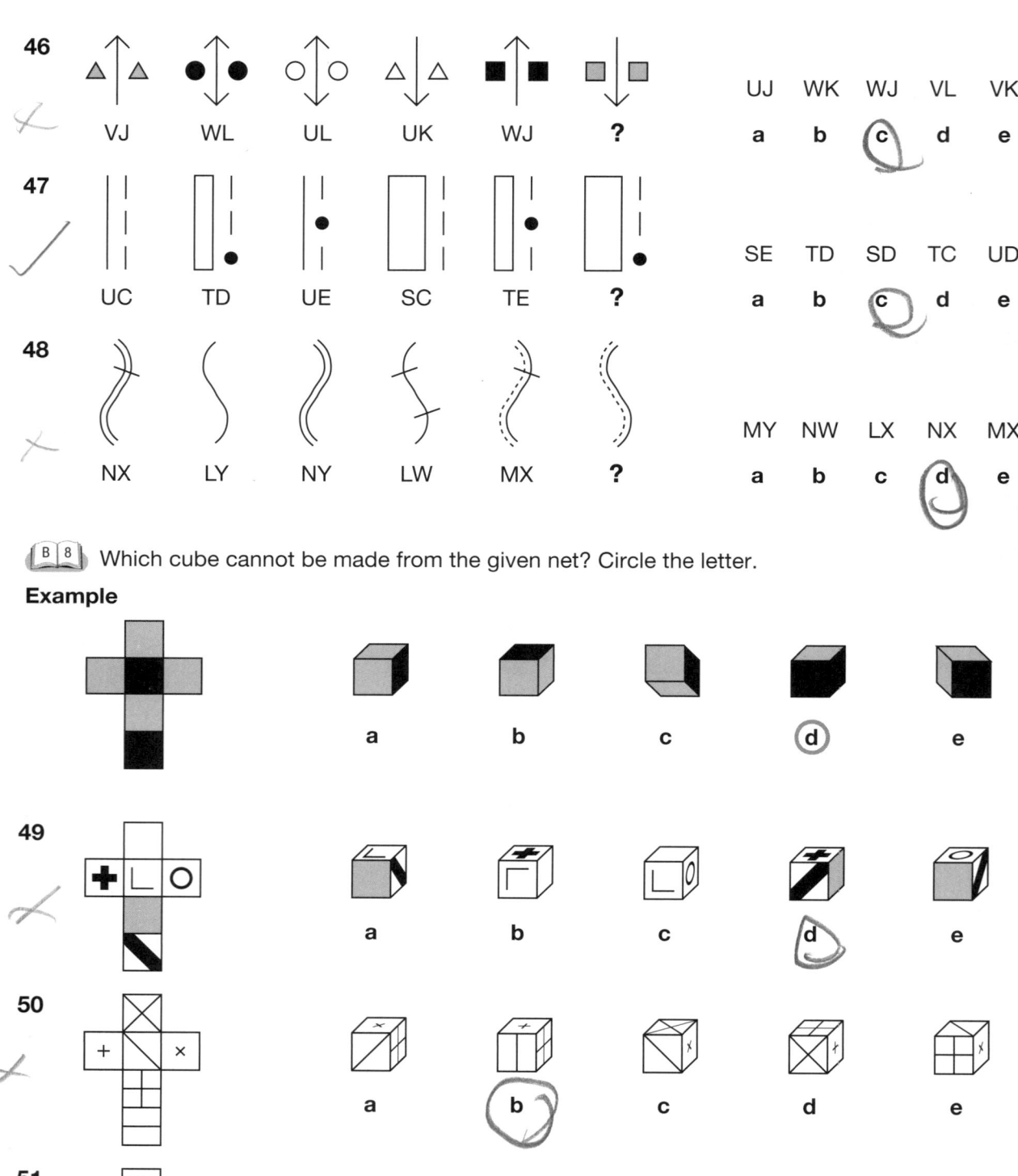

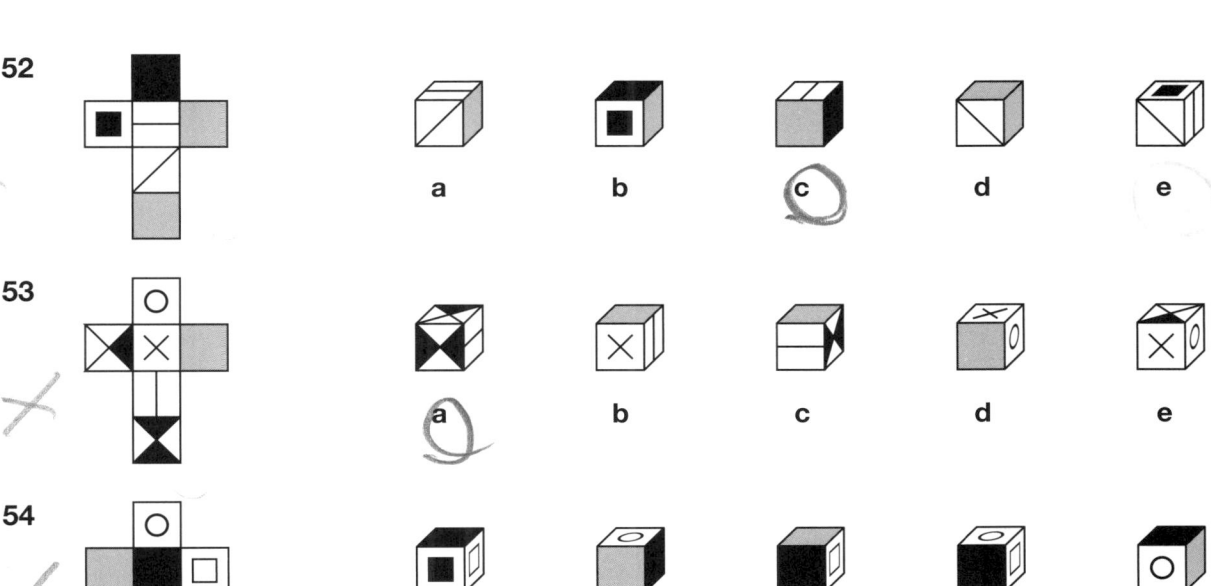
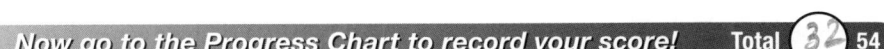

Progress Chart — Non-verbal Reasoning 9–10 years Book 2

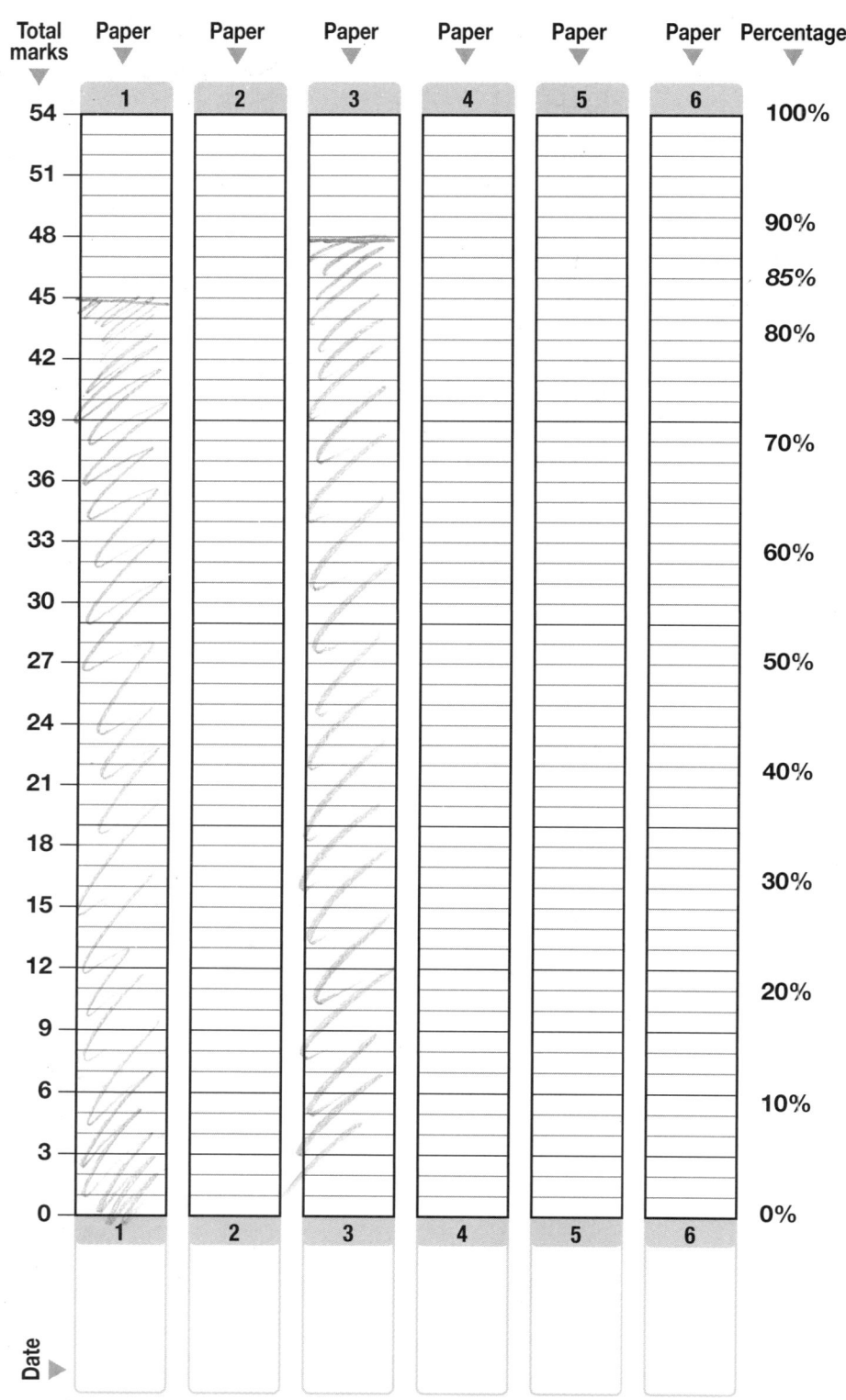